PICTURING SCOTLAND

THE LOTHIANS

NESS PUBLISHING

2 Linlithgow Loch and Palace, with St Michael's Church to the left of the palace. The Palace was built by James I after his return from exile in England, the work starting in 1425. Mary, Queen of Scots,

THE LOTHIANS

was born here on the 8th December 1542. The loch is home to a wide variety of birdlife and the path around the loch makes for a very pleasant walk.

Welcome to The Lothians!

Lying along the southern shore of the Firth of Forth, wrapped around Edinburgh, Scotland's capital city, The Lothians are something of a surprise package. There are few parts of Scotland where such a varied collection of fascinating places exists. You can visit sites of Neolithic ritual activity or board a supersonic airliner! Castles abound and stately homes are aplenty, yet all this site within an area little more than 50 miles from east to west and 15-20 miles from north to south. With the treasures of Edinburgh being so well known, it could be easy to miss what awaits discovery in the surrounding policies, so it is the aim of this book to sing loud for The Lothians and show something of the visual treats and historic locations that compete for attention when venturing outside the city.

The Lothians are made up of the three counties of West, Mid and East Lothian. While these names are relatively recent, their existence as administrative regions goes back much further. For example, East Lothian was Haddingtonshire until 1921, a name which first appeared (as *Hadintunschira*) in a charter of 1139, making it the earliest known sherriffdom (the forerunner of a county) south of the Firth of Forth. West Lothian was Linlithgowshire until 1924 and Midlothian was the County of Edinburgh until 1890.

The north grave at Cairnpapple Hill, described opposite. Originally covered by a stone cairn, it is now protected from the elements by a modern-day 'cairn'.

8   The Neolithic henge and Bronze Age burial site on Cairnpapple Hill near Bathgate in West Lothian. The henge bank is 60m/197ft in diameter. The north grave seen on p.7 can be inspected by

entering the cairn. In the distance on the right the Pentland Hills can be seen, which mark the southern boundary of Midlothian (see also pages 28/29).

10 Just down to the west of Cairnpapple Hill is the village of Torphichen, location of this fine church (actually called a 'preceptory') built by the Knights Hospitaller of the Order of St John of Jerusalem.

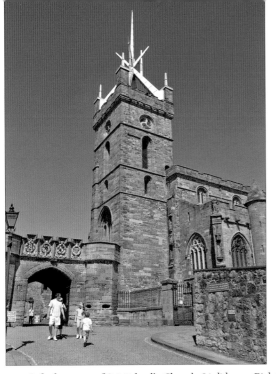

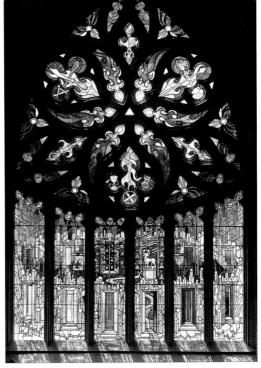

Left: the tower of St Michael's Church, Linlithgow. Right: in 1992 the church celebrated its 750th anniversary with the installation of this new stained glass window in the St Katherine's Aisle.

12 The Cross Well, Linlithgow, on market day. Remarkably, it was made in 1807 by a one-handed stonemason, as an exact replica of a previous well dating from 1535.

The Linlithgow basin of the Union Canal opened in May 1822, closed in 1965 and is now restored **13** to its former glory. Visit the Canal Museum and Tearoom or take a boat trip along the canal.

14 Just three miles north of Linlithgow is Bo'ness, which boasts the fine Kinneil House. It is situated in parkland which forms part of the Frontiers of the Roman Empire World Heritage Site.

The Bo'ness & Kinneil Railway runs for approximately five miles from Bo'ness to Manuel. **15**
Here, class D49 locomotive *Morayshire* departs from Bo'ness with a passenger service.

16 A few miles east of Bo'ness, Blackness Castle stands on the shore of the Firth of Forth. It is seen here from the hill on which the House of the Binns is situated (see p.19).

Built in the 15th century by the powerful Crichton family, its shape and location have led to it being referred to as 'the ship that never sailed'. This picture is taken from what might pass for the 'bow'.

18 From Blackness Castle we gain a first sight of two of the region's most famous landmarks, the Forth road and rail bridges. In this unusual view the two appear almost like one complex structure.

The House of the Binns stands as a living monument to one of Scotland's oldest families, the 19 Dalyells, who have lived here since 1612. It is open to the public in summer.

20 The Forth Railway Bridge, begun in 1883 and opened in 1890, seen here from the trackbed of the railway that served South Queensferry before the bridge was built.

What looks like a brave case of 'sail before "steam"'! However, the cruise liner Eurodam is at anchor, **21** discharging its passengers via the lighters that can also be seen, for a visit to South Queensferry.

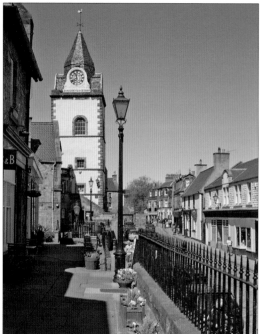

22 Although best known these days for its location between the Forth Bridges, South Queensferry is an attractive town in its own right. These two views look west and east along the High Street.

Its harbour also provides a view of great charm. The Queen referred to in the town's name is **23** Margaret, wife of King Malcolm III from 1070. She funded the first ferry.

24 The magnificent Hopetoun House is just a couple of miles west of South Queensferry. Charles Hope (later 1st Earl of Hopetoun) commissioned Sir William Bruce to build the original House in 1699

and work was largely complete by 1707. In 1721, William Adam was asked to remodel and enlarge the House; the frontage pictured here is his work. The back of the House is still Bruce's original.

26 Now moving just east of South Queensferry, this is Dalmeny House, designed by William Wilkins and completed in 1817. It is the home of the Earl of Rosebery.

Tucked away in the Edinburgh suburb of Balerno is Malleny Garden, renowned amongst other **27** things for its herbaceous perennials arranged with an eye for pleasing colour combinations.

28 The Pentland Hills rise to dominate the skyline south of Edinburgh. Several reservoirs have been created in the folds of these hills, of which Glencorse Reservoir is a particularly lovely sight.

The walk to the far end of Glencorse Reservoir offers this great view of the surrounding hills, which **29** are traversed by a network of paths. Inset: this dipper was busy in the burn.

30 The town of Penicuik nestles under the southern slopes of the Pentlands and contains a variety of architecture, such as these sturdy suburban villas with their unusual chimney stacks.

North-east from Penicuik we come to the village of Roslin. In recent years Roslin has been put firmly **31** on the world map thanks to the book *The Da Vinci Code* which features Rosslyn Chapel.

32 A visit to Rosslyn Chapel shows why it has captured the imagination of so many. The extraordinary quality, range and volume of the stone carvings are breathtaking. Left: the Apprentice Pillar; right: a Greenman.

This is the Library of Arniston House, a magnificent William Adam, Palladian-style mansion set in beautiful **33** parkland between Roslin and Gorebridge. It has been home to the Dundas family for over 400 years.

34 The Scottish Mining Museum at Newtongrange, a short distance north of Arniston, is a 'must' for any visit to The Lothians. Left: the pithead winding gear. Right: the winding engine, the largest in Scotland.

A highlight of the museum is the reconstruction of the mining coalface, seen here, showing how **35** the pit operated in its latter years, complete with dramatic sound effects!

36 Dalhousie Castle dates from the 13th century and was the home of the Ramsay family. Today it is a luxury hotel, a stay at which is an excellent way to engage with Scotland's history.

A few miles south of Dalhousie, Borthwick Castle is another example of fortress-turned-hotel. In its **37** 600 years it has seen plenty of conflict – the walls still bear the scars of Cromwell's cannons.

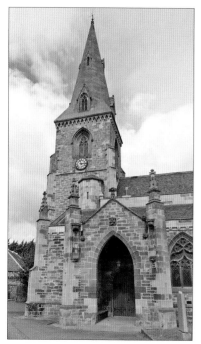 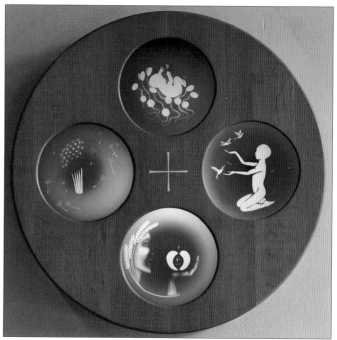

38 Left: St Nicholas' Church in the Midlothian town of Dalkeith. Right: inside the church, the beautiful Magnus Macintosh Memorial is cast crystal and depicts the four seasons of man.

Newbattle Abbey, Dalkeith. It has an unusual claim to fame for an abbey, in that the Cistercian monks 39
who lived here in the 12th century were possibly Scotland's first coal miners!

40 Now we leave Midlothian for East Lothian, setting the scene with this rural and maritime panorama. From Bransly Hill at the eastern end of the Lammermuir Hills, this view looks north across the mouth

of the River Tyne and on to the Bass Rock out in the Firth of Forth. The Kingdom of Fife can be seen in the distance, at least 25 miles away.

42 Left: Musselburgh, three miles east of Edinburgh, has plenty of interesting architecture like this domed and multi-sided house. Right: a 17th century sundial in Inveresk Garden, formerly at Pitreavie Castle.

Another scene from Inveresk Garden in Musselburgh. Within the stone walls of this hillside garden **43** are many unusual and exotic plants. A restored Edwardian conservatory and aviary also feature.

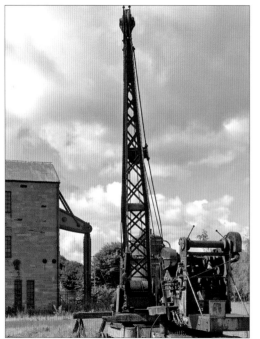 

44 Left: Prestongrange Museum provides a window onto East Lothian's industrial past. Right: A short
distance east is Prestonpans with its ruined but imposing six-storey tower built in the 15th century.

An attractive and unusual feature of the village of Prestonpans is its collection of murals which adorn **45** several buildings. This fine one is dedicated to the honour and memory of Prestonpans ancestors.

46 Another short hop eastwards and we come to Seton Collegiate Church, a haven of peace and tranquillity. Its story begins in the 12th century, when the site was chosen for a new church serving

the parishioners of Seton. The churchyard also contains the picturesque ruins of the Priests' houses, around which a small stream is channelled and is a lovely place to simply sit and enjoy the calm.

48 Moving a few miles inland, Glenkinchie Distillery offers site tours and an exhibition. This may look like a picture of the actual Still House but is in fact one of the superb models to be seen in the exhibition.

An aerial view of Lennoxlove House, which dates back to the 1300s. Having recently undergone extensive restoration, the house has regained its former glory. It is owned by the 16th Duke of Hamilton. **49**

50 Only a mile north of Lennoxlove is Haddington, East Lothian's county town. This is Court Street, with the steeple of the 1742-built Town House prominent.

Also in the piazza-like expanse of Court Street is this fine fountain, topped by a statue of Samson. A **51** settlement had been established by the year 1000; today Haddington's population is around 8,500.

52 This is St Mary's in Haddington, the largest parish church in Scotland. It is one of no fewer than 129 buildings in the town that are listed as historically interesting.

Haddington is built on the River Tyne and Nungate Bridge, seen here, is an early crossing point. **53**
King Alexander II, who reigned from 1214-1249, was born in Haddington in 1198.

54 The pretty village of Gifford is about four miles south of Haddington. The Mercat cross is on the left, with the Goblin Ha' Hotel beyond. This was named after the dungeon of nearby Yester Castle.

Yester Parish Church, Gifford, can be glimpsed through this array of autumn colours (the tower can **55** be seen opposite). The village takes its name from the Giffords of Yester Castle.

56 We return briefly to Haddington for this autumn view that takes in Lady Kitty's Doocot on the left, with Nungate Bridge visible on the right.

58 South of Haddington and Gifford, the Lammermuir Hills form a high plateau across which runs East Lothian's southern border. This wintry aerial view looks down on Whiteadder Reservoir.

Returning to East Lothian's coastal reaches, the small town of Gullane developed as a resort and **59** is known throughout Scotland for its championship-standard golf courses.

60 Dirleton is one of Scotland's great castles. This impressive cluster of towers – including the imposing keep at the south-west corner – is among the oldest castle architecture surviving in Scotland.

Dirleton has long been famous for its gardens. As well as these beautifully laid out lawns and flower beds, **61** it also boasts the 'longest continuous herbaceous border in the world' (Guinness Book of World Records).

62 North Berwick is the major seaside resort in The Lothians, not surprisingly with beaches like this. In the late 19th century it was branded as the 'Biarritz of the North' and became a magnet for 'society'.

Outside of summer the sea can of course show a very different face, but stormy days make for **63** equally interesting scenes.

64 North Berwick harbour. The earliest mention of a port at North Berwick was in a charter of 1177, when the pilgrims' ferry crossed to Fife. A herring works was established in 1642.

Gardens in the centre of North Berwick. **65**

66 A landmark visible from miles around, North Berwick Law is a volcanic plug – a remnant of solidified lava which is now all that remains of a volcano that once stood here.

The Bass Rock is another volcanic plug, but one that looks all the more dramatic as it rises sheer **67** from the sea. It is a sanctuary for seabirds, many thousands of which nest upon it.

68 A couple of miles east of North Berwick, Tantallon Castle is a formidable stronghold set atop the cliffs. It was the seat of the Douglas earls of Angus and endured many sieges in its active life.

South of North Berwick, the National Museum of Flight at East Fortune airfield houses a large collection of **69** historic aircraft, including this Concorde airliner. The airfield was built during the First World War.

70 East from East Fortune, we arrive at the lovely village of East Linton on the River Tyne.
The fast-flowing river provided the power for mills which provided employment in past times.

Among the many decorative touches in the village is this fountain in The Square, **71**
embellished with cherubim.

72 Looking very different from the picture on p.58, Whiteadder Reservoir provides the Lammermuir Hills with a place of recreation as well as water supply. The dam is virtually on the border with

the county of the Scottish Borders that lies to the south of East Lothian and the outflow runs into Borders.

74 Returning to East Linton, this is Preston Watermill, preserved in working order by the National Trust for Scotland. These buildings date from the 18th century and the mill was commercially active until 1959.

Just west of East Linton, Hailes Castle is a beautifully sited ruin incorporating a fortified manor of **75** 13th-century date, that was extended in the 14th and 15th centuries.

76 Our final move is to the historic town of Dunbar. These are the remains of the castle, in its heyday a two-part structure, one section (on the left) being on the mainland and the rest on a small island.

As well as showing the castle at a different angle (in the distance), this view gives an idea of the **77** complex harbour layout. It remains busy with a mix of pleasure craft and small fishing boats.

78 Left: a statue of John Muir, the man recognised as the father of the modern conservation movement, who spent his early life in Dunbar. Right: John Muir's birthplace, now a museum of his life.

Left: Dunbar Town House. Right: The Girl and the Swan statue. Overleaf: Dunglass Collegiate Church, **79** where East Lothian meets the Scottish Borders, which will be the subject of another tour in this series ...

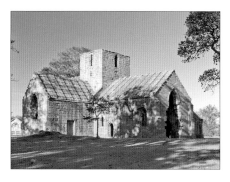

Published 2011 by Ness Publishing, 47 Academy Street, Elgin, Moray, IV30 1LR
Phone 01343 549663   www.nesspublishing.co.uk

All photographs © Colin and Eithne Nutt except p.32 (both) © Rosslyn Chapel Trust; p.33 © Arniston House;
p.49 © Crown Copyright RCAHMS; p.58 © Guthrie Aerial Photography; p.78 © East Lothian Museum Service

Text © Colin Nutt
ISBN 978-1-906549-13-8

Front cover: sunset at North Berwick; p.1: Red Row cottages at Aberlady; p.4: at Annet House Museum, Linlithgow;
this page: Dunglass Collegiate Church; back cover: Linlithgow Loch

For a list of websites and phone numbers please turn over >

Websites and phone numbers (where available) for principal places featured in this book in order of appearance:

Linlithgow: www.linlithgow.com/
Linlithgow Palace: www.historic-scotland.gov.uk (T) 01506 842896
Crichton Castle: www.historic-scotland.gov.uk (T) 01875 320017
Cairnpapple Hill: www.historic-scotland.gov.uk (T) 01506 634622
Torphichen Preceptory: www.historic-scotland.gov.uk (T) 01506 653733
St Michael's, Linlithgow: www.stmichaelsparish.org.uk
Linlithgow Canal Centre: www.lucs.org.uk (T) 01506 843194
Kinneil House: kinneil.wordpress.com
Bo'ness and Kinneil Railway: www.srps.org.uk (T) 01506 825855
Blackness Castle: www.historic-scotland.gov.uk (T) 01506 834807
House of the Binns: www.nts.org.uk (T) 0844 493 2124
Forth Bridges: www.forthbridges.org.uk
Hopetoun House: www.hopetoun.co.uk (T) 0131 331 2451
Dalmeny House: www.dalmeny.co.uk (T) 0131 331 1888
Malleny Garden: www.nts.org.uk (T) 0844 493 2123
Roslin: www.roslinvillage.com
Rosslyn Chapel: www.rosslynchapel.com (T) 0131 440 2159
Arniston House: www.arniston-house.co.uk (T) 01875 830515
Scottish Mining Museum: www.scottishminingmuseum.com (T) 0131 663 7519
Dalhousie Castle: www.dalhousiecastle.co.uk (T) 01875 820153
Borthwick Castle: www.borthwickcastle.com (T) 01875 820514

THE OLYMPIAN GAMES
IN WENLOCK:
A Pictorial History

This book is dedicated to all the Wenlock Olympians, past and present, who have worked hard to ensure the Wenlock Olympian Society and its Games have survived and thrived.

THE OLYMPIAN GAMES
IN WENLOCK:
A Pictorial History

Joy Sims & Ina Taylor with Catherine Beale

Ellingham Press
2012

British Library Cataloguing in Publication Data
A catalogue record for this book is available from the
British Library

ISBN 978-0-9570781-0-9

Ellingham Press
43 High Street, Much Wenlock, Shropshire TF13 6AD

Cover and book design by eMC Design Ltd
www.emcdesign.org.uk

Printed and bound in Great Britain by Graphics & Print,
Telford, Shropshire

CONTENTS

Introduction 7

The Vision of One Man 8
The Early Games 10
Tilting 12
The Pageantry 14
The Crowning Glory 16
Bringing in the Spectators 18
Women and Children 20
Sabin and the Cycling 22
The General Competition 24
Celebrating the Queen's Jubilee 26
The Games in Full Swing 28
Towards an International Olympic Games 30
A Carnival Atmosphere 32
Cecil Nevett (1891–1960) 34
Alfred Corfield (1900–87) 36

Games in the Forties 38
The 1950 Centenary Games 40
The Fifties 42
The Archery Wapenshaw 44
Jumping 46
Sixties Slow-down 48
The 1977 Revival 50
Live Arts 52
Disabled Sports 54
Produce, Handicraft & Art Show 56
The 100th Games 58
Fencing 60
Sporting Additions 62
National Recognition 64
Jimmy the Marathon Man 66

Women and Children Invited to Take Part 68
International Recognition 70
Equestrian Events 72
The Olympian Trail 74
Running 76
Shooting 78
Some Team Games 80
Other Sports 82
The Wenlock Pentathlon 84
Norman Wood (1921–2005) 86
Dedicated Supporters 88
Wenlock Greets the 2012 Olympics 90
The Olympic Impact 92
A Bright Future 94

Acknowledgements 96

INTRODUCTION

In the history of the Olympic movement in Britain, 2012 is a special year: it sees London becoming the first city in the world to host three Olympic Games. Simultaneously the people of Much Wenlock will be ever more in the spotlight as they hold their 126th Wenlock Olympian Games.

In 1850 the founder of the Wenlock Olympian Society, Dr William Penny Brookes, organised the first Wenlock Olympian Games for the local inhabitants, rich and poor and young and old alike, or as he himself put it, 'for every grade of man'.

From this local beginning the Wenlock Olympian Games spread their influence far beyond Shropshire to attain national significance. Brookes then urged the Greek people to revive the ancient Greek Olympian Games. His dream of an international Olympian Games became reality following on from the visit of Baron Pierre de Coubertin to the Wenlock Olympian Games in 1890. Inspired by what he had seen in Much Wenlock de Coubertin took up the torch and lit the flame when the modern Olympic Games as we know them were born in Athens in 1896, sadly just four months after the death of William Penny Brookes.

The Wenlock Olympian Games continued after the death of Brookes, and this book appropriately highlights the efforts of the dedicated band of volunteers who have carried on these cultural and sporting activities in Much Wenlock first established over 160 years ago.

In recent years the unique history and traditions of the Wenlock Olympian Society and its Games have been increasingly recognised locally, nationally and internationally. The unveiling of the mascot called *Wenlock* for the London 2012 Olympiad confirmed that the story of Brookes and the Wenlock Olympian Society would take its rightful place in Olympic history.

Thus is fulfilled the vision of Brookes, who wrote in 1867:

> Sow a single seed of a rare plant in the most secluded spot and if the soil and other conditions are favourable to its germination, it will grow up and bear other seed and, in time, produce plants sufficient to cover the length and breadth of the land.

The people and events depicted in this book match up to the pronouncement of the founder of the modern Olympic movement, Baron de Coubertin, in 1897 that

> The Wenlock people alone have preserved and followed the true Olympian traditions.

Chris Cannon
Archivist
Wenlock Olympian Society

THE VISION OF ONE MAN: DR WILLIAM PENNY BROOKES
(1809-95)

It is acknowledged that the international Olympic movement owes a debt to a doctor from a small market town in Shropshire. Dr William Penny Brookes not only set up a local games but his national and international campaigning led directly to the foundation of the International Olympic Committee and its first Olympic Games at Athens in 1896.

Although the Olympic Games are Brookes's international legacy, locally this Victorian physician is best known for improving the living conditions for inhabitants of the town of Much Wenlock and the wider Borough of Wenlock, Shropshire. Through his travels on horseback to patients around the town and in the outlying countryside, Brookes saw for himself the grim reality of working people's lives and considered what civic changes might improve their health and wellbeing. Unlike others, he not only initiated projects but was prepared to use his own money to get them moving. He also enlisted support from his other patients, the landed gentry, to bring his projects to fruition. The list of improvements he initiated is remarkable, including roads and sanitation, bringing the railway and gas lighting to the town, building a school and a corn exchange.

Brookes perhaps differed from some Victorian philanthropists in being equally concerned to improve the mind as well as the body of the borough's inhabitants. The building above the Corn Exchange (1853) should, he believed, have 'a large and handsome room for lectures or public meetings with an additional room for your library and a house for the librarian'. This was to be the home of the Wenlock Agricultural Reading Society, established in 1841 'for the promotion and diffusion of useful information'. Initially the library held books to educate local farmers on agricultural improvements but this was soon extended to include natural history and geology. Classes in music and art followed. In an effort to widen its appeal to agricultural labourers, Brookes introduced an Olympian Class in 1850 to benefit 'the Working Classes by the encouragement of outdoor recreation and by the award of prizes annually at public meetings for skill in Athletic exercises and proficiency in intellectual and industrial attainments'. The Wenlock Olympian Games had begun and the first meeting was held that year.

▲
The monument to Brookes in Holy Trinity Church, on the opposite side of the road to his house.

Dr William Penny Brookes (1809–95), a Shropshire physician, who is acknowledged as the father of the modern Olympic movement.
▼

▲
The Corn Exchange, built in 1853 at Brookes's instigation, demonstrates his concern for both the minds and bodies of the people in the Borough of Wenlock. Downstairs provided an area for trading and upstairs a library and meeting rooms for adult education. This would become the headquarters of the Wenlock Olympian Society as it is today.

THE EARLY GAMES

The first Games took place over two days, Tuesday and Wednesday 22 and 23 October 1850, and were held on the town's racecourse which offered a flat, open space set up for spectators. To engage the interest of local inhabitants, Brookes arranged a fine spectacle in the form of a procession through the town to the racecourse with band, flag bearers, athletes and committee. On the first day it is thought cricket, football and some foot-races took place with more running, high- and long-jumping, hopping and quoits held on the Wednesday.

Buoyed by the success of the first Games, Brookes and the committee added further events such as hurdles, archery and an evening dance the following year. Prizes were increased and the committee looked for an altenative venue to cater for the growing interest in the Games. They settled on a field below the disused windmill variously called the Windmill Field; the games field; the Linden Field (after the lime trees Brookes planted in 1869) and the Gaskell Field (in honour of the benefactor who in 1935 gave the field to the town for recreation).

Photographed on Tuesday 5 June 1867 at the beginning of the Games, this picture shows what an excellent natural grandstand was afforded by Windmill Hill. Arranged behind the carriage are the tilters, the band and games officials. A grandstand and marquees can be seen on the far left. This is believed to be the world's earliest photograph of a sporting event.

This 1860 poster shows the final year the Games were a part (or class as Brookes called it) of the Wenlock Agricultural Reading Society. Guest of honour, Lt-Col. Sir Herbert Edwardes, suggested renaming them 'The Shropshire Class of British Work and Play'. Instead Brookes preferred the Wenlock Olympian Society.

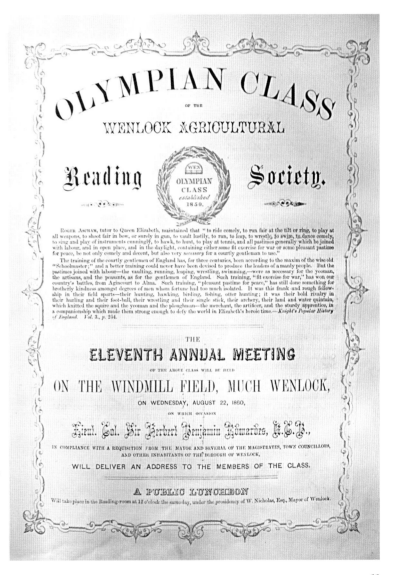

OLYMPIAN CLASS

OF THE

WENLOCK AGRICULTURAL

Reading Society.

OLYMPIAN CLASS established 1850.

Roger Ascham, tutor to Queen Elizabeth, maintained that "to ride comely, to run fair at the tilt or ring, to play at all weapons, to shoot fair in bow, or surely in gun, to vault lustily, to run, to leap, to wrestle, to swim, to dance comely, to sing and play of instruments cunningly, to hawk, to hunt, to play at tennis, and all pastimes generally which be joined with labour, and in open place, and in the daylight, containing either some fit exercise for war or some pleasant pastime for peace, be not only comely and decent, but also very *necessary* for a courtly gentleman to use."

The training of the courtly gentlemen of England has, for three centuries, been according to the maxim of the wise old "Schoolmaster;" and a better training could never have been devised to produce the leaders of a manly people. But the pastimes joined with labour—the vaulting, running, leaping, wrestling, swimming,—were as necessary for the yeoman, the artisans, and the peasants, as for the gentlemen of England. Such training, "fit exercise for war," has won our country's battles, from Agincourt to Alma. Such training, "pleasant pastime for peace," has still done something for brotherly kindness amongst degrees of men whom fortune had too much isolated. It was this frank and rough fellowship in their field sports—their hunting, hawking, birding, fishing, otter hunting; it was their bold rivalry in their hurling and their foot-ball, their wrestling and their single-stick, their archery, their land and water quintain, which knitted the squire and the yeoman and the ploughman—the merchant, the artificer, and the sturdy apprentice, in a companionship which made them strong enough to defy the world in Elizabeth's heroic time.—*Knight's Popular History of England. Vol. 3, p. 254.*

THE

ELEVENTH ANNUAL MEETING

OF THE ABOVE CLASS WILL BE HELD

ON THE WINDMILL FIELD, MUCH WENLOCK,

ON WEDNESDAY, AUGUST 22, 1860,

ON WHICH OCCASION

Lieut. Col. Sir Herbert Benjamin Edwardes, K.C.B.,

IN COMPLIANCE WITH A REQUISITION FROM THE MAYOR AND SEVERAL OF THE MAGISTRATES, TOWN COUNCILLORS, AND OTHER INHABITANTS OF THE BOROUGH OF WENLOCK,

WILL DELIVER AN ADDRESS TO THE MEMBERS OF THE CLASS.

A PUBLIC LUNCHEON

Will take place in the Reading-room at 12 o'clock the same day, under the presidency of W. Nicholas, Esq., Mayor of Wenlock.

TILTING

Whilst Brookes's inspiration for the Games came from the classical world, it was also honed by the fashion for medievalism so beloved of his contemporaries, the artist Burne-Jones and poet Tennyson.

The chivalric vision of the knight and his lady found a place in Brookes's Games when in 1858 he introduced tilting at the ring. Riders, mounted with lance in hand, would charge full tilt along the course aiming to pierce a small ring suspended from a cross bar. The victorious 'knight' would bend the knee before his lady to receive the olive crown (a laurel wreath) and have the yellow sash emblazoned with the words 'Honour my Guide' placed across his chest. All this was to the strains of a 'Prize Ode' sung by the choir.

The 'knights' were often the sons of local farmers because Brookes had stipulated the event was only open to persons residing within ten miles of the Guildhall. Contestants were dressed for the part in a loose tunic, white breeches, riding boots and a flat cap.

The contest started in true chivalric style: 'The Knights of the Lance having assembled opposite the grand stand, the champion ... [from last year] threw down his gauntlet, which was taken up by one of the competitors and handed to each of the others.' Brookes then addressed them: 'Gentlemen tilters your position is indeed a proud and enviable one, privileged to contend for these splendid prizes, the gifts of the noble and the fair, and for those olive crowns, emblems of ancient Greece...'

Tilting was such a crowd-pleaser that Brookes introduced tilting over hurdles in 1869. Each competitor galloped along the course, jumped two hurdles and then aimed their ten-foot metal-tipped spear at the ring.

In 1900 there was a brief attempt to add tilting at the ring on bicycles, but this never caught on because it lacked the panache of the equestrian version. After the First World War tilting on horseback resumed briefly, but times had changed, and the event was dropped through lack of interest.

▲
The hurdles can be seen in the background of this 1887 photograph as John Webster gallops through. The cross beam also doubled up as the finishing post for races.

◀ The Ainsworth family from Spoonhill Farm near Much Wenlock produced an impressive dynasty of tilting champions. Here twenty-two-year-old Charles Ainsworth, farmer and auctioneer at the town's cattle market, poses with cups, medals and laurel crown after becoming champion tilter over hurdles in 1875.

Charles Ainsworth, winner of both flat tilting and hurdle tilting in 1887, bends his knee before the Queen of Beauty, Miss Marion Serjeantson, to receive the sash and laurel wreath. He will also be presented with the champion's cup (far left) donated annually by the Forester family. Dr Brookes can be seen with the herald standing on the right.
▼

THE PAGEANTRY

In 1859, a year after Brookes successfully brought tilting to the Games, he added a little more pageantry with the introduction of the herald, a feature of the ancient Olympics. A young boy on a white pony would head the procession through the town to the games field. Behind the herald, eight small boys would carry the laurel wreaths followed by two mounted pages bearing the silver cups to be awarded.

To bring suitable pomp and ceremony to the herald's role, Brookes commissioned a special outfit. Turning to the costume department of Covent Garden theatre, Brookes requested details of the correct tournament costume worn at the time of Henry VIII. Thus the herald wore 'a green silk velvet tunic, richly embroidered with gold, over which was thrown a crimson mantle. He wore also white buckskin trousers, with buff leather boots piped with red; also a blue silk velvet cap, turned up with crimson, and carried the silver decoration of the class, enriched with a silver garter with the motto of the class, an elegant white plume rising out of a silver encasement.' The costume was ordered and paid for by Brookes.

Continuing his chivalric theme Brookes gave the title Queen of Beauty to the young lady chosen annually to crown the champion tilter. She epitomised the lady for whose favour the knight competed. Various daughters of local dignitaries and supporters of the Games, ranging in age from eleven to their early twenties, were given the honour. They were also permitted four maids of honour. In the early twentieth century, the Queen of Beauty became the May Queen and in 1950 she was renamed the Carnival Queen, but retained her entourage of young maidens.

▲
The medieval flavour of Brookes's early games can clearly be seen in this painting where the herald stands alongside the champion tilter at the edge of a pavilion for jousting. Both wear garments harking back to earlier times.

The pomp and ceremony remained well into the twentieth century.

15

THE CROWNING GLORY

This photograph on the right has had a hard life, but its survival is extraordinary. Hand-coloured and framed, it was presented to Thomas Jukes by the Wenlock Olympian committee in 1871 'as a mark of their respect and gratitude for his untiring exertions in furtherance of the success of the Society'. At some point during the intervening hundred and forty odd years, the photograph has suffered light damage. Nevertheless it depicts in extraordinary detail the climax of the 1867 Games.

The photograph carried the caption 'The Queen of Beauty, Miss Wadlow, presenting the Cup to the Victor in the Tilting Match at the Ring, Wm Gregory, at the Wenlock Olympian Games, on Whit Tuesday, June 11th 1867'.

Dr Brookes can be seen in the centre wearing the Wenlock Olympian Society's own medal he has been presented with. Next to him is the Queen of Beauty little Minnie Wadlow flanked by her four maids of honour. She has just crowned William Gregory, the champion tilter, with the 'olive crown' and presented him with 'a silver goblet value £7'. Gregory was a local man who had also won the tilting in 1858, in its year of introduction. Despite moving to Birmingham, Gregory regularly returned to Wenlock to compete in the Games.

The young boy standing to the far right of the picture is thirteen-year-old William Tench, son of a local quarryman. The newspaper described him as 'a small boy on a small pony who rode about the field with all the self complacency of the older competitors. From the commencement of the contest the sympathy of the spectators was decidedly with this little fellow; and as he gave evidence of considerable skill in the wielding of his lance, he was greeted with hearty applause each time he flew under the cross-bar. The riding was rapid, and never were there sharper efforts made to get first to the ring.' He proved a very popular winner of the second prize and was awarded 'a handsome silver mounted hunting whip, with richly enchased handle value £2 10s', which he is holding.

we have followed the noble and highly appreciated example of the ancient Greeks, by conferring upon the victor in our most popular contest, Tilting at the ring, the much prized olive crown, enhanced however in its value, and consecrated by the Ceremony of Coronation by a lady's hands.

▲
Brookes explains in a letter what he intended with the crowning ceremony.

BRINGING IN THE SPECTATORS

As one of the directors of the Wenlock & Severn Junction Railway Company, Brookes played a major role in bringing the railway to Much Wenlock because he believed the town's future prosperity depended upon it. It offered a practical way of transporting limestone from the local quarries and livestock to and from the town's market, not to mention the benefits to passengers. In 1861 the line opened and it was hoped this would coincide with the Games on 23 October, so notices were posted advertising cheap fares that day. However, Victorian 'health and safety' threatened to derail Brookes's plans when it transpired the Board of Trade Inspector needed to travel the line to ensure its safety. Not one easily put off by officialdom, Brookes managed to secure an agreement that 'a special train should run from Shrewsbury taking such ladies and gentlemen as had confidence in the security of the line; from the steadiness of the train, and the care taken by the staff concerned the possibility of an accident was very remote.'

The first train brought participants and spectators to the Wenlock Games. As it pulled up alongside the platform the Wenlock Juvenile Band (formed by Brookes) played 'See, The Conqu'ring Hero Comes!'. The procession of herald and tilters was lined up ready to escort the first passengers to the games field.

When the line opened, this pavilion was the original railway station; it was then replaced in 1864 by the stone-built one. Brookes had the wooden structure moved to the games field and recycled as a pavilion for the bowling club. It stands in exactly the same place today and fulfils the same role.

An early photograph of railway coaches standing in the station at Much Wenlock soon after it opened. Brookes ensured that the station was sited next-door to the games field, not in the centre of the town as originally discussed.

The football team stands outside Much Wenlock railway station. Football, initially with 14-a-side, was on the programme of the early games but disappeared in the 1860s. One member of this team appears to be dressed for tilting with riding boots and a tilter's cap.

19

WOMEN AND CHILDREN

Most events in the Wenlock Olympian Games were intended for men. Sports for women were virtually unknown in Victorian England, although in the second Games in 1851 Brookes included a race for 'old women' to compete for 'woman's much-loved herb' – a pound of tea. The 'elderly' winner was forty-five-year-old Mary Speake, a labourer's wife from the town. The local newspaper reported that the competitors 'acquitted themselves remarkably well, considering the disadvantage under which they laboured in not being provided with the "Bloomer costume" attired in which they would have run capitally.' Second prize was claimed by 'old woman' Anne Meredith, a thirty-eight-year-old charwoman who received a smaller ration of tea.

Although women racing for tea was a one-off Olympian sport, more ladylike competitions appeared in the Games. Prizes were awarded for 'the quickest and best knitting' and 'the neatest and best sewing'. In 1868 a girl at the National School won a workbox (value 7/6) for knitting a pair of stockings, and her adult counterpart received pieces of material to make a gown. Schoolgirls were encouraged to take part in poetry recitation and educational pursuits like reading, spelling, Bible history, English history and drawing.

Brookes wanted the boys at the National School to take part in running and jumping events as part of his efforts to get physical education into the school curriculum to improve children's health, but this never included girls. They could not compete in the Olympian Games until 1921, when girls' 100 yard and 120 yard flat races were added. Women would have to wait until the 1950s before they could compete in flat races, and it was not until 1978 that the full range of athletic events was open to them.

▲ Children from the National School, which Brookes helped found, were encouraged to take part in the games: boys in the running and girls in the handicrafts. Competitions existed for both to win prizes for their learning.

NATIONAL
OLYMPIAN ASSOCIATION.

CIVIUM VIRES CIVITATIS VIS.

PRESIDENT:
The Right Honourable The Earl of Bradford

FOURTH FESTIVAL, HELD AT MUCH WENLOCK
MAY 25TH & 26TH, 1874.

First Prize for *Knitting*
awarded to
Hannah Sandell
PUPIL OF THE WENLOCK NATIONAL SCHOOL.
W P Brookes.
Hon. Secretary.

◄ Twelve-year-old Hannah Sandell, daughter of one of the town's blacksmiths, won a book about flowers as first prize for her knitting. The book plate was personally signed by William Penny Brookes.

The girls' role in the games was largely to look pretty and carry baskets of flowers in the procession. Dancing at the end of the day was considered a suitable female activity.

SABIN AND THE CYCLING

Brookes continually sought new and exciting additions to the Games and in 1876 introduced cycle racing. It began with a three-mile race involving eight laps of the Linden Field. Cycling was still in its early days and only four contestants came forward, from Coventry, Birmingham, Wolverhampton and Bridgnorth, but none from Wenlock. Thomas Sabin, a farmer from Allesley near Coventry, delighted spectators with his 'speedy performance' in taking first prize in the 1876 Games. He had first purchased his 'ordinary', as the penny-farthing bicycle was known, three years earlier, joined the Coventry Bicycle Club, and started racing the following year.

The second year of cycle racing at the Wenlock Olympian Games saw the introduction of a one-mile race as well as a three-mile and subsequently a half-mile race. Like tilting, cycling had its fair share of incidents. There were collisions between cyclists and spectators. One competitor in 1887 'fell soon after the start through colliding with a lady who got on the track, and got his machine doubled.' Falling off the machine was an occupational hazard and there are various reports of Sabin coming off, then remounting, pedalling like fury and still taking first place.

Once introduced in 1876, cycling remained a popular fixture at the Games, and, in the twenty-first century, vintage cycle racers on penny-farthings and other early bicycles wow the crowds much as they did in Brookes's day.

Cycling was such a crowd-pleaser at the Games that it featured on the front cover of several 1890s programmes.

▲ Vintage cycle races at the Olympian Games in the 21st century delight spectators.

◄ Thomas Sabin, winner of the 1876, 1877 and 1878 three-mile cycle races and of the one-mile in 1877 and 1878 at Wenlock, stands proudly alongside his penny-farthing.

WENLOCK
Olympian Games

(UNDER A.A.A. AND N.C.U. RULES),

On Whit-Tuesday, May 26th, 1896.

President : LYDE BENSON, Esq.

Handicapper : MR. W. W. ALEXANDER.

Starter : MR. W. ROBERTS.

Judges : MR. F. HALE,   MR. T. BARNETT,
MR. E. PRICE,   MR. C. E. AINSWORTH.

Referee : MR. W. LAWLEY.

Hon. Treas. : MR. F. SARJEANT.

Secretary : MR. W. LAWLEY.

Competitions and
Names of Competitors.

PROGRAMMES 2D. EACH.

W. LAWLEY, PRINTER, MUCH WENLOCK.

THE GENERAL COMPETITION

Brookes continued to develop his Olympian Games and in 1868 introduced the General Competition. Recalling the classical Olympic Games, Brookes was reviving the pentathlon, although with sports more suited to those already in the Wenlock Games. His General Competition involved putting the (36lb) shot, running high leap, running long leap, climbing a 55-foot rope and running the half-mile.

By this time, the Wenlock Olympian Games were attracting athletes of high calibre from far afield and Brookes wanted to ensure they remained interested in competing, so a handsome prize for the General Competition was created: the Nike medal. Eighty-four pounds and four shillings (equivalent to £3,735.72) was spent on the creation of the medal die with a further £14 (equivalent to £621.88) paid out for each silver medal made. This was a huge sum of money for the time and demonstrates Brookes's commitment to attracting the best possible athletes.

Never losing sight of his original aim, namely to encourage Wenlock inhabitants to become fitter and healthier, Brookes also brought in a local version of the General Competition restricted to athletes living within the Borough of Wenlock. Events in this category were foot racing, hurdling, standing long leap, javelin and throwing the hammer. The local winner the first year was Thomas Barnett, licensee of the Swan & Falcon in the High Street. His prize was a gold scarf pin.

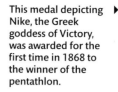

This medal depicting Nike, the Greek goddess of Victory, was awarded for the first time in 1868 to the winner of the pentathlon.

▲ Warren FitzWarren from Market Drayton won the very first pentathlon in 1868. He is seen here wearing the newly-minted Nike medal. He competed successfully for a year or two, then served on the Olympian Society's committee.

The pentathlon at Wenlock attracted athletes from around the country, and Henry Brooke (no relation to William Penny Brookes) from the German Gymnasium in London carried off the first prize in 1869 and 1870. The impressive display of medals on his jacket indicates what an outstanding athlete Brooke was.

In 1923 Harold Langley, competing for Sparkhill Harriers, won the pentathlon at the Wenlock Games. The following year he represented Great Britain in the triple jump in the 1924 Paris Olympics (often referred to as the *Chariots of Fire* Olympics). This represented a landmark for the Wenlock Olympian Games because he was the first of their athletes to compete in the international Olympic Games.

Langley displaying ▶ his Wenlock Olympian Society pentathlon medal after the 1923 Games.

CELEBRATING THE QUEEN'S JUBILEE

Queen Victoria's official Golden Jubilee celebrations were on 20 and 21 June 1887; although the annual Games would be a few weeks early, the Wenlock Olympian committee dedicated their thirty-eighth Games to Her Majesty. A thirty-foot oak tree, donated by Lord Wenlock, was planted on the games field, its roots watered in with champagne poured from the prize tilting cup – the winner of the flat and hurdle tilting that year was Charles Ainsworth, who is seen being crowned on that occasion on page 13. As Brookes poured the champagne, he asserted jovially, 'Had the Chancellor of the Exchequer known of this custom, he would, I feel assured, have exempted all the members of the Wenlock Olympian Society from the additional duty on imported bottled champagne, in consideration of the laudable object for which it is used at these festivals.'

The names on the adjacent poster are interesting and show the involvement of the town in the games. The Ainsworths, outstanding tilters, can be seen serving on the committee alongside other local farmers like Jukes and Wadlow. Lawley, stationer and printer whose home and business was a few doors away from Brookes, serves as referee, treasurer and secretary to the Society as well as printer of this poster; whilst licensee of the Royal Oak in Barrow Street, that outstanding athlete William Roberts (see page 29), is the starter. Thomas Barnett, licensee of the Swan & Falcon in the High Street and winner of the first pentathlon (local category) in 1868 (see page 24), assists in the judging.

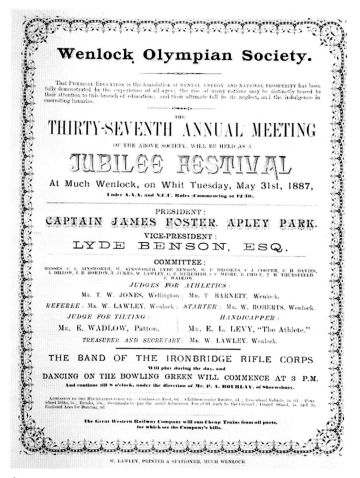

Familiar names appear on this notice of the 38th Olympian Games but one name here links the Wenlock Olympian Games with the International Olympic Committee's first Olympic Games in Athens in 1896. E.L. Levy would in nine years' time appear at the very first international Olympic Games. Levy travelled to Athens intending to compete in the weightlifting but ended up judging the competition.

At the start of the 1887 Games the herald, ten-year-old Thomas Yates, takes centre stage on his white pony. Dr Brookes, resplendent with his Olympian and Gymnastic Society medals, stands to the right in this photograph which was taken to mark the Jubilee Festival. Vice-President Lyde Benson is on Brookes's left. Tilters John Webster, Richard Webster and Charles Ainsworth are mounted behind the officials holding their lances aloft. Flags and standards show up against the skyline and add to the pageantry of the occasion.
▼

THE GAMES IN FULL SWING

There is an air of anticipation in the grandstand as everyone looks towards the Bensons from Lutwyche Hall who are about to present the prizes. Mrs Benson is holding the flowers as she steps down into the ring. Lyde Benson was President of the Wenlock Olympian Society from 1894 to 1896 and one of Brookes's most steadfast supporters.

▼

From 1877 to 1882 F.B. Harrison (from Barrow) livened up the Wenlock Olympian Society, both as a committee member and an athlete. In 1877 he took first in the 200 yards 'in splendid style', then the quarter-mile flat race in 1878 and the hurdles the following year, not to mention a long jump of 19' 10" (6.05m) in 1880. At the same time he was a very energetic committee member who drummed up interest in competing amongst the locals. In 1877 he is credited with bringing twenty new competitors into the games. He also served the games as starter and handicapper as well as promoting amateur athletes in the Wenlock Olympian Society, being President in 1878.

William Roberts was a Much Wenlock publican who was an exceedingly good athlete in the 1860s. In the Olympian Games he came first in high jump, long jump and hurdles. He also served on the committee and was a starter at the Games for over fifty years. He can be seen in front of the grandstand to the left, wearing a watch chain. Roberts's sporting prowess was not restricted to the games field: he was described as 'a good all-round cricketer and had many fine batting performances to his credit, for which he was the recipient of several cricket bats', not to mention being a good shot and figuring prominently on the prize lists at pigeon shoots around Shropshire.

Richard Preece poses here with his lance after winning the flat tilting. Typical of the tilters, he was a farmer's son who competed in his late teens and early twenties, taking first place in 1877 and 1880 and second in 1879. After that he settled down to assist in farming his father's 500 acres at Cressage, a few miles from Wenlock.

TOWARDS AN INTERNATIONAL OLYMPIC GAMES

Once the Wenlock Olympian Games were established, Brookes tried hard to extend the idea to a National Olympian Association. Not only did Brookes dream of a national event, he had his sights set on international games and looked towards Greece, homeland of the classical games. His correspondence with the Greek king produced some interest and the donation of a silver cup in 1877, but not the impetus for international co-operation Brookes sought.

A notice in *The Times* in 1889, placed by a Frenchman proclaiming the 'advantages of athletic sports and games and their physical, social and moral effects on education', caught Brookes's attention. An exchange of letters between the eighty-year-old doctor and twenty-six-year-old Baron Pierre de Coubertin began. Despite their age difference both men shared the vision of an international Olympic games.

Brookes invited de Coubertin to the 1890 Games in May but the Frenchman was unable to attend; nevertheless he agreed to visit Much Wenlock in October that year. A second shorter Games with only seven events, but containing highlights like the tilting, was arranged in his honour. Despite a rainy day, the traditional Olympian procession assembled at the top of the High Street headed by the herald in costume on his white pony leading the Ironbridge Volunteer Band, followed by Brookes and de Coubertin, the Wenlock Olympian Society committee, schoolchildren in suitably festive garb, mounted tilters and the Shropshire Yeomanry Cavalry. This was a spectacle designed to impress. The procession entered the games field through a decorated arch of evergreens and dahlias with 'Welcome to Baron Pierre de Coubertin and Prosperity to France' emblazoned in blue, white and red upon it. Speeches followed, a tree was planted with a champagne libation on its roots and then the Games began.

The visit was an inspiration to de Coubertin and their joint vision led directly to the first international Olympic Games in Athens in 1896. Sadly Brookes died four months before the Games, but de Coubertin later wrote: 'The Wenlock people alone have preserved and followed the true Olympian traditions.'

This medal, presented to the Wenlock Olympian Society by de Coubertin following his visit in 1890, was awarded to the tilting champion the following year (see page 71).

De Coubertin and Brookes exchanged photographs prior to the 1890 visit, and this is the one the young Frenchman sent to Much Wenlock.

20 rue Oudinot
Paris. Avril. 21. 1891

My dear Dr Brookes

Very many thanks for your letter.
I am sorry to say that there is n't
any chance of my attending the
forty first annual Festival of the
olympian Society, for we have on
Whit monday an International Meeting
here in Paris. Besides the competition
for the national championship will begin
on May the 14th & end only on the 6th
of June when the Paris Colleges will
have their annual four-oared races
on the Seine. Every thursday & Sunday
send him your instructions. His name
is: J. J. Tusserand.

I am delighted to hear that a
challenge cup of £50 has been given to
the olympian Association.

Wishing you every success & hoping
to see you again before long, I remain,
Dear Dr Brookes
Ever yrs very faithfully

Pierre de Coubertin

Remember me, please, to your daughter
& Grand daughter. I am most thankful
for their kind "Souvenir".

31

A CARNIVAL ATMOSPHERE

Even late in the 1890s competitions had entered the Games for things like the best decorated bicycle. Women who had been given no real part in the Games took up such challenges with alacrity, so by the beginning of the twentieth century a carnival element had developed. Newspapers reported 'decorated go-carts', clowns mounted on donkeys and nursery rhyme characters like Red Riding Hood and the Old Woman Who Lived in a Shoe in the procession.

From the outset the band played an essential role in the opening procession, initially at its head but, once the herald was introduced, following immediately behind. Although Much Wenlock had its own band, the town band was by no means assured of a place in the procession because the job of providing a band of sixteen men was always put out to tender and the committee took the lowest figure. In 1929 when they tendered £8, Oakengates tendered £6 and Jackfield £9, so it is obvious who led the procession from the Gaskell Arms Hotel down the High Street that year!

▲ Decorating the float and taking part in the opening procession to the Olympian Games was the annual highlight for many in Wenlock.

◄ The Much Wenlock Town Band in 1901. Members were in their twenties and thirties, all lived and worked in the town with jobs ranging from postman, quarryman, house painter to shop assistant. Here they are dressed in their Sunday best (some even sport tail-coats) and wear a buttonhole for the Olympian Games. 'His Master's Voice' sits in front. The band met at the Royal Oak pub in Barrow Street whose proprietor was Olympian athlete William Roberts (see page 29).

▲ Although described as a decorated mail cart, this 1907 float bears a remarkable resemblance to a perambulator. It is thought the girl is standing in the George Shut, an alleyway alongside the George & Dragon pub.

CECIL NEVETT
(1891-1960)

One of Wenlock's successful home-grown talents of the early twentieth century was Cecil Nevett, son of a local bricklayer. After leaving school Cecil set himself up as a boot repairer at 26 High Street, the family home. At 5′ 7½″ (1.71m) and lightly built, weighing 9 stone, he took up sprinting in his spare time along with younger brother Herbert. Herbert restricted himself to competing in the Wenlock Olympian Games, coming second to Cecil in the 120 yards in 1914. This was an admirable achievement because by 1914 Cecil was a well-known Midlands athlete. As a member of Birchfield Harriers, he had won the County Sprint Championship in 1912 and taken third in the high jump that year.

Even the First World War failed to stop Cecil. He won races for his battalion in Italy and Egypt, then in India he won an army pentathlon (consisting of the 100 yards, 220 yards and 400 yards flat races, high jump and long jump), by taking four firsts and a second. All of this was excellent preparation for competing in the Wenlock Olympian Games on his return. The Games revived in 1921 after a break for the First World War and in 1922 the thirty-one-year-old local favourite took second prize in the pentathlon which consisted of high jump, long jump, shot put, 220 yards and half-mile hurdle. This was the pinnacle of Nevett's achievements in Wenlock though he continued competing for Birchfield Harriers in the Midlands and further afield.

In 1924 Nevett became a postman at Much Wenlock and supported the Wenlock Games both by stewarding and as a judge for the foot-races.

In the mid 1950s Cecil Nevett was still taking an active part in the games as a judge. He can be seen in a dark suit (front row) with other stewards and committee members on the games field. A young Norman Wood can be seen in shirt sleeves.

Cecil Nevett in 1914 poses in his running spikes wearing the badge of the Birchfield Harriers club. He grips corks, with strings attached to prevent them being dropped. Some athletes at the time believed this improved their performance.
▼

▲
Nevett on the left with fellow postman Percy Langford. Cecil proudly wears his athletics medals and displays on the table in front some of his athletics prizes. What fascinated many people about this athlete was that he was a chain-smoker!

ALFRED CORFIELD
(1900-87)

Born into a family of foresters in Homer, near Much Wenlock, in 1900, Alf Corfield showed athletic promise from an early age. Although Alf's sprinting was good enough to win the under-15s 200 yards in the 1913 Olympian Games, jumping was his real love. That began one day in the woods working alongside his uncle who cut a long straight ash pole and showed the lad how to use it to leap over hedges. Alf was soon honing his hedge-vaulting in his spare time. By the age of twelve he was good enough to win a watch (value 10/-) with an eight-foot pole vault. Although he always claimed later in life he wasn't fit enough to be a runner, he still won several 100 and 200 yard races in his early teens.

By 1921 Alf was making a name for himself at the pole vault and decided to buy the best vaulting pole. He sent to Harrods for a bamboo pole which cost him two weeks' wages (50/-) and later he bought a pair of spiked running shoes, also from Harrods. In 1921 he took third prize at Wenlock with 8' 8" (2.64m) and first prize the following year with 8'11" (2.72m). Pole vaulting disappeared off the Olympian Games programme, so Alf never jumped there again but he had already moved to bigger meetings. At the peak of his jumping career, in the mid 1920s, he was travelling around the Midlands by train with his two 16-foot poles (a spare was always needed), labelled 'to be called for', in the guard's van. During the 1920s he won four gold and three silver medals at AAA competitions and recalled attending meetings where there were outstanding runners like Harold Abrahams (the 1924 *Chariots of Fire* 100m gold medal-winner) but as Alf put it, 'I was the jumper.'

Alf proudly displays one of his original bamboo poles bought from Harrods that cost him two weeks' wages. He continued working as an highly-skilled tree-feller well into his seventies.

With his pole vaulting days over by the age of thirty, Alf competed as a runner for many years. He took second in the men's over-45s 100 yards flat at the 1954 Olympian Games. He was presented with a special Olympian medal in 1986 in recognition of his outstanding athletic career.

IRONBRIDGE COMRADES

SPORTS

in the
REGATTA FIELD, IRONBRIDGE,
on
TUESDAY, AUGUST 7th, 1923,
Commencing at 1 p.m.

ADVANCE TICKET - - 1/-.

Alf clearing the bar to take first prize and win a barometer at Ironbridge. He was jumping around eleven feet and recalled how hard the landing was in those days without mats. To avoid injury, he said you had to land on your feet.

37

GAMES IN THE FORTIES

The Olympian Games were beginning to lose their appeal to athletes in the early 1930s and at their committee meeting after the 1932 Games, the committee decided not to stage a games the following year due to lack of interest. 'Wenlock's Shame' trumpeted the headline of the local paper when this was announced. Although the Games ceased, the carnival part of the procession remained hugely popular and continued until the outbreak of the Second World War.

In 1945, as part of the victory celebrations in the town, a games was planned. It was not officially a Wenlock Olympian Games but it is noticeable that the same names crop up as organisers and officials.

The carnival continued thereafter and in 1948 had a distinctly Olympic theme in recognition of the international Olympic Games coming to London.

MUCH WENLOCK AND DISTRICT

Victory Garden Show
Carnival, Sports, &c.

IN AID OF THE

RED CROSS AGRICULTURAL FUND
(Registered under the War Charities Act, 1940)

AUGUST BANK HOLIDAY
(MONDAY, 6th AUGUST, 1945)

LINDEN PLAYING FIELDS, MUCH WENLOCK,

PROGRAMME - - - PRICE 1/6

Adults will be admitted by this Programme only.

Children under 14 years pay at Gate, 6d.

Bridgnorth Journal Co.

▲
The link with the 1948 London Olympic Games can clearly be seen on the float carrying the Carnival Queen as it passes along Sheinton Street in the town.

The Olympic torch was carried by Harold Lloyd on the 1948 float. In 1953 he took gold in the pentathlon at the Olympian Games, which caused great delight. No local man had won gold since 1870. ▶

THE 1950 CENTENARY GAMES

Appropriately it was a discussion between Wenlock's physician, Dr F. W. Hudson Bigley, and the Town Clerk, George Matthews, that led to the Olympian Games being restarted to celebrate the centenary of Brookes's original Games. The pair decided to approach people who had organised the Victory Games in 1945 for help because many were also former Wenlock Olympian Society members. At the group's first meeting Dr Bigley was voted in as President and George Matthews as Honorary Secretary. When Matthews discovered the Wenlock Olympian Society had £250 left in the kitty, in addition to the trophies and medals, it was full steam ahead.

August Bank Holiday, then at the beginning of the month, was chosen as the date. Alongside the sports, plans were made for a big carnival and horticultural and handicraft events.

The sports offered in 1950 were on a modest scale: flat races, high jump, long jump, cycling and archery. In the spirit of Brookes's first Games there were children's races for those living in the parish of Much Wenlock and a relay race for children resident in the borough. For the first time women were invited to compete in 100 yards and 220 yards flat races and the archery. The colour and drama of the archery (see page 44) proved the highlight on the field. Because the Wenlock Olympian Society had not been active for almost twenty years, there were few local athletes around, but the 1950 Games were well supported by athletes from the Birmingham area and as far away as Manchester. People in the town threw themselves wholeheartedly into the carnival and the horticultural and handicraft shows.

▲
Dr Bigley (right), President of the Wenlock Olympian Society, receives an award in recognition of the part he played in reviving the Games in 1950. Honorary Secretary George Matthews, who also played a major role in the revival, is in the centre and David Williams, the society's Chairman, makes the presentation during the games.

Crowning the Carnival Queen in the town square at 11.30 a.m. signalled the start of the Games.
▼

▲ Local girl Honor Brazier took first with her collection of wild flowers in the under-10s.

THE FIFTIES

When the Games were revived in the 1950s they were accompanied by a lively carnival in which people of the borough eagerly participated. Thousands of spectators also came to Much Wenlock by train.

Wenlock Olympian Society.
— FOUNDED IN 1850 —

PRIZE SCHEDULE

FOR THE

CORONATION YEAR ATHLETIC SPORTS

— ON —

AUGUST MONDAY

(AUGUST 3rd, 1953)

COMMENCING AT 2 P.M.
AT THE FAMED
Linden Playing Fields, Much Wenlock
(The Birthplace of the Olympic Games)

* * * * *

£130

VALUE IN PRIZES

Also the Pentathlon Medal
Two Challenge Cups
and One Silver Plaque

offered in a most complete sporting programme of

**8 Junior and 7 Senior Events
3 Ladies Events
3 Cycle Events**

(under A.A.A. & W.A.A.A. Laws and N.C.U. Rules)

* * * * *

Hon. General Secretary :
A. G. MATTHEWS,
Corn Exchange, Much Wenlock, Shropshire.

Slater & Co., Printers, Iron-Bridge.

WENLOCK OLYMPIAN SOCIETY
(FOUNDED IN 1850).

Horticultural & Handicrafts Show

on LINDEN PLAYING FIELDS, MUCH WENLOCK

AUGUST MONDAY, 1957

SCHEDULE OF OPEN CLASSES

JUDGES :
Horticulture—Mr. H. G. Phillips (Buildwas Park) and A. N. Other.
Handicrafts—Mrs. A. Dykes and Mrs. K. B. Whitfield.
Cookery and Preserves To be appointed.
Woodwork—Mr. T. Shapter.   Art—Mr. F. H. Salter.

SECTION A.—VEGETABLES.

Class		Prizes 1st	2nd	3rd
		s. d.	s. d.	s. d.
1.	A collection of four kinds of Salad Vegetables, selected from the following : Beet, Celery, Cucumber, Endives, Lettuce, Seedling Onions, Radishes and Tomatoes	7 0	4 0	2 6
2.	Beet, globe type, four	5 0	3 0	2 0
3.	Cabbages, two	5 0	3 0	2 0
4.	Carrots, four	5 0	3 0	2 0
5.	Cauliflowers, two	5 0	3 0	2 0
6.	Lettuces, two	5 0	3 0	2 0
7.	Marrows, two	5 0	3 0	2 0
8.	Onions, six	5 0	3 0	2 0
9.	Peas, twelve pods	5 0	3 0	2 0
10.	Potatoes, six, round or oval	5 0	3 0	2 0
11.	Potatoes, six, kidney	5 0	3 0	2 0
12.	Runner Beans, twelve	5 0	3 0	2 0
13.	Dwarf or French Beans, twelve	5 0	3 0	2 0
14.	Shallots, twelve, large	5 0	3 0	2 0
15.	Shallots, twelve, small	5 0	3 0	2 0
16.	Broad Beans, twelve	5 0	3 0	2 0
17.	Tomatoes, six	5 0	3 0	2 0

FRUIT.
(Foreign Fruit disqualified)

18.	Apples, dessert, six	5 0	3 0	2 0
19.	Apples, cooking, six	5 0	3 0	2 0
20.	Currants, Black, Red or White, ½lb dish	5 0	3 0	2 0
21.	Gooseberries, twelve	5 0	3 0	2 0
22.	Raspberries, twenty-four	5 0	3 0	2 0
23.	Loganberries, twenty-four	5 0	3 0	2 0

The Baby Show was hugely popular. It had begun with just 'the bonniest baby' category but by 1959 had expanded into three classes: birth–6 months, 6–12 months and 12–24 months with 34 entrants. A 'prettiest mother' prize was also awarded.

WENLOCK OLYMPIAN SOCIETY
Annual Celebrations, Show & Sports 1959

BABY SHOW

FIRST PRIZE

AWARDED TO

Class No.

◀ Kenny Milner wins first prize for his sweet peas in the horticultural marquee in the 1953 Olympian Games. He was also awarded the blue ribbon for 'Best Exhibit in Show', which was a great achievement for a young boy competing against experienced gardeners in the borough.

▲ The carnival queen with her attendants was one of the most popular floats in the carnival. A dance was held in the town a few weeks beforehand at which the queen and her attendants were chosen.

WESTERN   BRITISH RAILWAYS   REGION

MUCH WENLOCK
Olympian Games and Carnival

Special Excursion Bookings

Monday, 4th August, 1958
TO
MUCH WENLOCK

FROM	DEPART			RETURN FARES (Second Class)
	a.m.	a.m.	p.m.	s. d.
WELLINGTON	11 10	11 22	12 50	2/3
KETLEY	11 16	11 31	12 58	2/-
KETLEY TOWN HALT	11 18	11 33	1 1	2/-
NEW DALE HALT	11 21	11 35	1 5	2/-
LAWLEY BANK	11 24	11 38	1 8	2/-
HORSEHAY AND DAWLEY	11 30	11 43	1 15	1/9
DOSELEY HALT	11 33	11 46	1 19	1/9
LIGHTMOOR HALT	11 37	11 50	1 23	1/6
GREEN BANK HALT	11 40	11 53	1 26	1/3
COALBROOKDALE	11 43	11 56	1 31	1/3
BUILDWAS	11 51	p.m. 12 6	1 36	1/3
FARLEY HALT	12 0	—	1 44	-/6
	p.m.	a.m.	p.m.	
MUCH WENLOCK arr.	12 5	12 19	1 50	—

PASSENGERS RETURN SAME DAY BY ANY TRAIN.

Children under Three years of age, Free; Three and under Fourteen years of age, Half-fare.

RETURN TRAINS CALLING AT ALL STATIONS AND HALTS TO WELLINGTON

WILL LEAVE MUCH WENLOCK at 5-45 P.M., 7-5 P.M. and 8-0 P.M.

IT WOULD ASSIST THE RAILWAYS IN PROVIDING ADEQUATE ACCOMMODATION IF INTENDING PASSENGERS WOULD OBTAIN THEIR TICKETS IN ADVANCE.

THE ARCHERY WAPENSHAW

With Brookes's nod towards medievalism in the early Games, it is not surprising to find that archery featured in the second Games of 1851. That year local man Richard Felton, an ostler living in the High Street, won the archery as well as the quoits, but thereafter archery does not seem to have been a sport people wanted to compete in and by the 1860s it had vanished from the programme. Although the Wenlock Olympian Society committee talked optimistically about reintroducing archery once the tennis lawn had been extended, the event did not reappear for ninety years.

The 1950 Centenary Games provided the impetus to put archery firmly back on the programme with the Wenlock Hunting Horn given as a trophy for the Annual Challenge Competition. Since there was no archery club in the Wenlock borough, assistance with organising the contest was sought from retired Group Captain Moore and the Wolverhampton Company of Archers. He set up the archery wapenshaw (using an Old English term for a 'weapon show' at which groups were invited to display their weaponry – a term Brookes would surely have approved of!) and invitations were issued. This proved extremely popular with clubs arriving from Sheffield, London, Leicester and Essex as well as Shrewsbury for the first wapenshaw. The real seal of approval came with the appearance of Miss Barbara Waterhouse, the World Lady Champion. Thereafter archery went from strength to strength and a disabled archery contest was introduced in the 1980s.

When members attending the Games brought their children along, a junior archery class was added. At one of these in 1981 ten-year-old Alison Williamson competed and won a silver medal. By winning bronze at the 2004 Olympic Games she became the first athlete from the Wenlock Games to win a medal at the international Olympics.

The Wenlock Olympian Society has always been extremely proud of the part the Games played at the outset of Alison Williamson's national and international career. She is seen here as a ten-year-old competing in 1981 at the Wenlock Olympian Games.

Alison has competed at every Olympic Games since 1992 and is seen here with the bronze medal she won in the 2004 Athens Olympiad. As the first person from the Wenlock Olympian Games to win a medal in the Olympics, Alison Williamson is the fulfilment of William Penny Brookes's vision.

The 1950 archery contest took place on the games field followed by an invitation to the public to participate in a supervised 'balloon-bursting' and 'William Tell' contest ('Three arrows for sixpence'). Actually it wasn't 'health and safety' that moved the archery off the Gaskell Field to the neighbouring Cutlins Field where this photograph was taken in 1952 but the building of the new secondary school.

JUMPING

'Leaping in height' and 'leaping in distance' were Brookes's terms for the two major jumping events in the early Games with a cord instead of a bar being used initially for the high jump. No mats were used. Competitors landed directly on bare earth which required plenty of skill to prevent injury. 'Make sure you land on your feet' was the tip because diving over or flopping was sure to lead to injury. The results were incredible: in 1870 Londoner Henry Brooke, the pentathlon winner at Wenlock (see page 24), jumped 5' 3" (1.60m), almost his own height, to win.

Olympian athlete Jimmy Moore (see page 66) remembers being at the Wenlock Games when he first saw the Fosbury Flop used to clear the high jump. At the time everyone in Wenlock was taught to use the scissors-jump to clear the bar. Payne, an athlete from Birchfield Harriers, arrived to compete and sailed over in a completely new way. 'You can't jump like that, do it again properly,' the Wenlock judges told him. So he dived over the next time, clearing it once more and was promptly disqualified because he couldn't do the scissors-jump.

Today the Olympian Games has high jump, long jump and triple jump with events in most categories for children as well as adults.

Twenty-year-old Edward Sandells, the local greengrocer, jumped 4' 8" (1.42m) in 1880 to take the high jump prize that year.

Pole leapers, as they were called, sit in the foreground of this early photograph c.1880. The bar they jump is visible behind them and so is a ladder resting against the tilting bar.
▼

47

SIXTIES SLOW-DOWN

At the beginning of the 1950s various national events were cause for celebration and gave momentum to the Wenlock Olympian Games; there was the Festival of Britain in 1951 and the Coronation in 1953. In the fifties there was excellent attendance from most of the athletic clubs around the Midlands. In addition to the carnival procession, which was the highlight of the year for the townspeople, there were numerous sideshows on the games field like coconut shies, bowling for the pig, skittles, a baby show, a 'Grand Show of flowers, fruits, vegetables, preserves, toys and handicrafts' in the large marquee, and exhibitions of maypole and country dancing: in fact all the fun of the fair, all on the same day and frequently taking place on the same field.

But as the fifties moved into the sixties, the committee had to work hard to sustain interest in the sports. New events were introduced like American double tennis, a gymkhana, even bob-apple racing, but entries dwindled and by the end of the sixties the Wenlock Olympian Games had ceased. The same was not true of the carnival and fancy dress parades which had originally heralded the Games. These were more popular than ever and took on an independent life of their own.

▲ Parents watch their children streak past them in this late 1950s photograph of the Games.

◀ In 1960 Michael Sagar became the last herald to take part in the Wenlock Olympian Games. He wears the original herald's regalia that Brookes commissioned and is mounted on the traditional white pony. As his uncle Jasper Moore leads him down the High Street, the band behind him is just passing Ashfield Hall.

WENLOCK OLYMPIAN SOCIETY

BOROUGH OF MUCH WENLOCK 1468 - 1968
QUINCENTENARY CELEBRATIONS

GRAND GALA DAY

TO CONCLUDE THE CELEBRATIONS

Gaskell Recreation Ground, Much Wenlock
on SATURDAY, 3RD AUG., 1968

CROWNING OF QUINCENTENARY QUEEN & PRINCESS
will take place in the Square at 1-45 p.m.

CHILDREN'S SPORTS
(SPECIAL ENTRY FORMS)

CHILDREN'S FANCY DRESS COMPETITION
(NO ENTRY FORM REQUIRED) — THREE CLASSES FOR GIRLS AND THREE FOR BOYS. — Ages 3 – 5 yrs.; 6 – 10 yrs.; 11 – 15 yrs.

MAMMOTH HORTICULTURAL AND HANDICRAFTS SHOW
(SPECIAL ENTRY FORM)

Fairground Organ . Punch & Judy . Amusement Fair
Pony Club Demonstrations . Sheep Dog Demonstrations
Five-a-Side Football Match . Comic Dog Competition
MAYPOLE DANCING . BALLOON RACE - ROAD SAFETY DISPLAY
SIDESHOWS GALORE !   REFRESHMENTS
Fancy Dress Wheelbarrow Race through Town at 7-30 p.m.

FINALE DANCE & BARBECUE at British Legion Hall 9 p.m.

Ground open at 1 p.m. Admittance to Ground : Adults 2/- ; Children 1/- ; Ample Parking Cars 1/-

Entry Forms from — SPORTS Mr. J. P. DAVIES Secondary Modern School, Much Wenlock, Shropshire.
HORTICULTURAL AND HANDICRAFT SHOW The Corn Exchange and local shops.
All enquiries to either Mr. A. G. MATTHEWS, Wormer House, Much Wenlock Mrs. H. MONKS, 15 Southfield Road, Much Wenlock

▲ This 1968 poster highlights the tensions beginning to be felt as sports and carnival jockey for prominence.

THE 1977 REVIVAL

With the Queen's Silver Jubilee on the horizon, Wenlock Mayor John Simpson (1976–7) and Deputy Mayor Norman Wood discussed how the town might celebrate it. As a former PE teacher at the local secondary school, Norman was keen to revive the athletics, especially for children. As a Cambridge Blue, John too was very enthusiastic about reviving the Wenlock Olympian Games. A meeting was called for anyone and everyone who wanted to revive the Games.

Interested parties were invited on the committee; gone were the days of waiting to be proposed and seconded. The vital qualifications were enthusiasm and energy.

The previous Games had been on August Bank Holiday Monday which was at the beginning of August, but in 1965 the bank holiday was moved to the end of August, which didn't suit the gardeners, and so they organised a produce show on a separate weekend from the Games.

The date for the 1977 Games was fixed by the national Silver Jubilee celebrations as Whitsun Bank Holiday at the start of June, but the following year it was decided to put the Games into a weekend in July, before the schools broke up and people took their holidays, but after the main exams.

The Silver Jubilee Games were not exactly Olympian Games although the Wenlock Olympian Society donated the medals and every competitor received a Jubilee Crown. The sports consisted of athletics, along with swimming and diving in the new school pool. The sports started for the under-sixes and went up to under-14s. This being the 1970s girls as well as boys were allowed to compete. New events were five-a-side football, rounders for the Cubs and Brownies and an indoor five-a-side hockey match. The only competitions open to adults were a 'Special Parents Knock-Out' event and a tug-of-war for which clubs and pubs were invited to submit teams.

As in previous Games, the Saturday started with the crowning of the Carnival Queen at lunch-time followed by a carnival procession to the Linden Field ready for the opening of the athletics at 2.20 p.m. Shops, businesses and houses decorated their windows for the Jubilee weekend. A barbeque and disco dancing rounded off the evening.

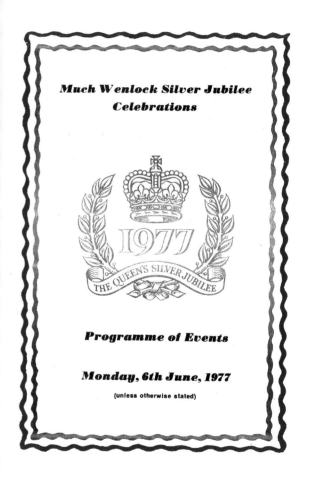

Much Wenlock Silver Jubilee Celebrations

1977

THE QUEEN'S SILVER JUBILEE

Programme of Events

Monday, 6th June, 1977

(unless otherwise stated)

LIVE ARTS

Soon after the 1977 Games came another event in the spirit of Brookes's original Olympian class whose objective was to promote 'the moral, physical and intellectual improvement of the inhabitants of the town and neighbourhood of Wenlock, and especially of the working classes, by the encouragement of outdoor recreation and by the award of prizes annually at public meetings for skill in athletic exercises and proficiency in intellectual and industrial attainments'.

The first Live Arts event took place on a Saturday in May 1980 with categories for drama, music and verse. This event was aimed at schoolchildren, and half of the classes were restricted to those living in the catchment area of the William Brookes School; in Brookes's day the boys' events had been restricted to children attending the National School in the Bull Ring. To encourage children to take part it was agreed from the outset that all entrants would receive a certificate showing they had participated, and there would be a first (£1.50), second (£1) and third (50p) prize in addition to a trophy for each category.

As time went on one Saturday was never enough to accommodate all the entrants even when the 40-minute play was dropped, and evenings during the preceding week were taken up. At its height in 1999 the event was every evening of the preceding week and all day Saturday – a mammoth task for the volunteers.

Categories within Live Arts have evolved over time with music, poetry and prose remaining constant. In 2011 the creative writing section offered the chance to prepare a 2½ minute podcast of airtime with the Prime Minister or local MP and in 2012 dance appeared on the programme.

▲

Medals and trophies are awarded in the Live Arts Festival. In addition to trophies for specific events, the committee introduced some for Endeavour, Musicianship and the Olympian of the Year to recognise the huge effort some children put in even though they might not take first in any of the events they entered.

School entries are popular.
▼

From humble beginnings in 1980 the event now spreads over a number of days. The WOS logo in the left-hand corner acknowledges how much a part of the Olympian Society the arts are.
▼

Live Arts FESTIVAL 2010

William Brookes School, Much Wenlock

Wed 10th
and
Fri 12th March
from 5.30pm
and
Sat 13th March (*Primary School ages only*)
from 9am to 6pm

Admission Evening sessions £1 Saturday all day £2 Children free

Closing date for entries – Friday 12th February 2010

DISABLED SPORTS

In 1980 table tennis for wheelchair athletes was introduced into the annual Games along with archery for disabled athletes. In the case of the archery able-bodied and disabled athletes were able to compete side-by-side. Following its success, a much enlarged programme of sports for the disabled came into the Olympian Games and was supported by the Bridgnorth Beavers and the Shrewsbury Sharks, two local groups working with disabled athletes. At its height the Games had events like swimming, trampolining, javelin (one for precision and one for length), shot put, discus, skittles, slalom wheelchair racing and even a wheelchair sprint for disabled athletes. Team games like badminton, basketball, football and netball for the disabled also formed part of the Olympian Games during the 1980s and nineties. The disabled athlete who had shown the most endeavour and enthusiasm in the Games that year was awarded the Wenlock Olympian Cup.

Late in the 1990s funding for care assistants to support disabled athletes was withdrawn, which meant sadly that 1998 was the last time sports for disabled athletes formed part of the Wenlock Olympian Games.

▲ Patrick Hill was selected to carry the flag in the Special Olympics.

Athletes from ▶ Bridgnorth Beavers limber up on the games field.

◀ Wenlock swimmer Patrick Hill trained with Shrewsbury Sharks every Thursday and, assisted by them, went on to compete internationally. He was chosen to represent Great Britain in the under-25s Disabled Games in Belgium in the 1970s where he won a silver medal.

During the 1980s ▶ the Wenlock Olympian Society had a flourishing programme of events for disabled athletes.

HANDICAPPED EVENTS TIMETABLE		
11.00	TABLE TENNIS	GYMNASIUM
11.30	SHOT	FIELD
	JAVELIN (distance)	FIELD
	DISCUS	FIELD
	JAVELIN (accuracy)	FIELD
11.30	WHEELCHAIR RACES AND SLALOM	FORECOURT
12.30	SWIMMING	POOL
2.00	SKITTLES	GYMNASIUM
	TRAMPOLINE	GYMNASIUM
2.30	BADMINTON	SPORTS' HALL
	BASKETBALL (individual)	SPORTS' HALL
	TEAM EVENTS—5-a-side HOCKEY ..	SPORTS' HALL
	NETBALL	SPORTS' HALL
4.30	AWARDS AND PHOTOGRAPHS ..	MAIN HALL

Organiser: Mr. TED COWANS

The Bridgnorth Beavers athletic team, keen supporters of the Wenlock Olympian Games, with their coach. Local swimmer Patrick Hill (top right) trained with the Beavers every Saturday and swam in the disabled games at Wenlock.

PRODUCE, HANDICRAFT & ART SHOW

When the Games were revived in 1977 an eager band of helpers from the WI decided to revive the produce, handicraft and art element which had been a part of Brookes's original Games. Instead of marquees, the hall in the Secondary School was used. Later the event moved to the Priory Hall. This building would have been known to Brookes as the National School, and pupils from it in his day were encouraged to take part in the children's events in the Games. After the school closed in 1952, the building was used for storage and then transformed into a village hall for the town – the perfect venue for the produce, handicraft and art show.

Late in the 20th century the horticulture and handicraft element of the Games had lapsed. In 2011 there were sufficient keen gardeners, a gardening club in the town and a doubling of the allotment provision, to consider revival. Sustainable Wenlock, a group unknown in Brookes's day but one he would surely have commended, organised the 'Roots, Shoots & Fruits Show' in September 2011 in the Priory Hall. Outside on the church green that day a food festival was held.

Founded by Dr Penny Brookes in 1850

Produce, Handicraft and Art Show

Saturday 1st July 1995

Open to the public at 1.00pm
(Judging at 11.00am)

Priory Hall Much Wenlock

Secretary: Mrs V.Humphries, Tel 727684

Produce, Handicraft & Art Show

First Prize

Awarded to Joy Sims

Class 38. Shortbread.

The 'Roots, Shoots & Fruits Show' in 2011 was a modern revival of the produce show.

▲ Trestle tables were laid out inside the Priory Hall for handicraft exhibits.

◀ Laura Sims aged 11 displays her exhibits and certificates which won her the trophy in 1993.

▲ Trophies to be awarded at the Produce, Handicraft and Art Show are displayed in the Post Office window.

THE 100TH GAMES

The 100th Games in 1986 were celebrated in grand style. The guest of honour was Baron de Coubertin's great-nephew Monsieur Geoffroy de Navacelle. Plenty of other VIPs attended that year, keen to give the Wenlock Olympian Games recognition for its part in the revival of the modern Olympic Games because Birmingham was campaigning to host the 1992 Games. Denis Howell, former sports minister, who was leading Birmingham's bid, attended, along with other IOC and BOA representatives. Film crews from far and wide also appeared in the town, which gave Much Wenlock a small taste of what would happen once London 2012 was announced.

Quite apart from that the 1986 Games had attracted a record entry with close to 2,000 competitors travelling from as far afield as the Isle of Man. Many more turned out over the two days to watch the spectacle, which began with a relay of young athletes arriving with an original 1948 Olympic torch. Once presented to Monsieur de Navacelle, it was taken to the top of the Windmill Hill to light a rocket which exploded in the sky above the games field to announce the Games had begun.

▲
Officials of the Wenlock Olympian Society in 1986 pose with their guests.
L to R Mayoress Mrs Dorothy Brown, Mme Anne de Navacelle, Denis Howell MP,
Mayor Cllr George Brown, M. Geoffroy de Navacelle, Norman Wood (Secretary),
Mrs Joan Teece (Chairman), Cllr Ernest Higgs (President).

◀ Ernest Higgs holds a 1948 Olympic torch.

FENCING

The inclusion of fencing as part of the Wenlock Olympian Games is entirely down to two people: Ismay and Steve Cowen. They were already fencing coaches and in the early 1980s, whilst taking their children swimming in the town, were asked if they could offer fencing for children in the school holidays. This became so successful that a regular Thursday evening class followed and Norman Wood, inspirational reviver of the Olympian Games, asked the couple if fencing could be part of the Games. By 1985 the sport was firmly established on the programme, and their coaching has continued every week since.

Fencers can start as eight-year-olds and many stay on until they go to university. So popular is the fencing that parents and children travel from Herefordshire and the edge of Wales for the Thursday evening classes and of course take part in the annual Wenlock Olympian Games. The popularity is probably because from the outset the Cowens wanted fencing to be open to all children who would like to learn. That has meant working hard to find sponsorship and, in the early days, sometimes putting their hands in their own pockets to ensure the cost of the hall was met and there was enough kit available for children to borrow.

▲ Local girl Samantha Hill learned to fence with the Wenlock Olympians and went on to compete internationally. Seen here on the left, Sam was selected to compete in the World Cadet Championship in Italy where she got into the quarter-finals and was ranked 24th out of 160 in the world.

◀ This fencing display took place outside for the benefit of HM The Queen's visit in 2003 but that was exceptional. The fencing normally takes place in the sports hall.

A fencing match during the 2011 Games.

SPORTING ADDITIONS

Over the years various sports have come and gone as the Wenlock Olympian Society moved with the times to capture the interest of competitors and spectators alike. The earliest Games included sports which owed more to the village green than the classical games in Greece, events like climbing the pole, chasing the pig, jumping in bags, hopping and jingling (in which blindfolded competitors stumbled around in a roped-off area trying to catch the person ringing a bell and darting out of their way).

Quoits appeared in Brookes's first Games in 1850. They were made of iron by one of the local blacksmiths and said to be based on a horseshoe, so it is appropriate that the winner the first year was local ostler Richard Felton, who lived in the High Street. Quoits remained a competitive sport in the Wenlock Games until 1931, but when the Games resumed in 1950 quoits were absent. The sport reappeared occasionally in the 1980s, sometimes billed as 'The Ancient game of Quoits Championship', and was staged in 1990 when Princess Anne visited for the de Coubertin Games (see page 64).

With the prize nine gallons of beer, it is not surprising that the tug-of-war contest did not last very long as an Olympian sport! There were problems with drunkenness, broken glass on the field and damage from hefty boots.

The Karate Championships appeared at the Games as a Friday evening event in 1988 and remained on the programme for fifteen years. ▶

Quoits was extremely popular in the early part of the 20th century with men happy to practise behind the pub as they do here at the Horse & Jockey, known locally as 'The Bonnets'.
▼

Wheelbarrow races featured in the early Games and a variant, blind wheelbarrow racing, was also introduced to amuse the crowds.
▼

63

NATIONAL RECOGNITION

In 1990 a hundred years had passed since the visit of de Coubertin to the town to watch the Olympian Games they staged for him that autumn (see page 30). President of the British Olympic Society HRH Princess Anne attended the Games on the Saturday along with leading representatives of the British Olympic Association. This was very much the culmination of the efforts of two of the society's stalwarts, Ernest Higgs and Norman Wood, who had both worked hard to establish links with the national body.

The 1990 Games began on Friday afternoon with cricket, swimming and karate events and went on to fill the next two days. The princess attended on the Saturday when there was a full athletic programme, disabled games and the art and handicraft event in the Priory Hall. Quoits was revived along with 'putting the stone' (see page 82) where local quarrymen competed against each other in throwing a 35lb hunk of limestone rock. In keeping with the spirit of Brookes's original games, there was a children's poetry competition for a poem entitled 'Olympic Sport' and the princess awarded the prize.

On the Sunday a new event was introduced: the triathlon. This consisted of swimming, cycling 15 kilometres and a three-and-half-mile run.

64

◀ President of the Wenlock Olympian Society John Simpson, who along with Norman Wood had played such an important role in the 1977 revival of the Games, talks to Princess Anne.

Samantha Leigh, an outstanding multi-event competitor, at the Games in 1990. ▶

A demonstration of tilting ▶ was originally planned for these Games but it proved impossible to find a team kitted out and experienced enough to perform such a dangerous sport, so a professional jousting demonstration was laid on. It still proved extremely popular.

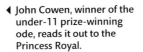

◀ John Cowen, winner of the under-11 prize-winning ode, reads it out to the Princess Royal.

JIMMY THE MARATHON MAN

In his late seventies, Jimmy Moore is one of the best-known and much-loved athletes of the Wenlock Olympian Games, immortalised in the mural that depicts twenty-first-century life in the town on the wall of the Priory Hall. Jimmy's marathon successes have been truly incredible, matched only by the amount of money he has raised for charity by running.

Although not Wenlock-born, most would consider him a son of the town; he was a Liverpool evacuee in 1941 who never returned to Liverpool. At the local National School he took part in 220 yard races, became flyweight boxing champion and played football. Longing to take part in the London Marathon, Jimmy bought himself some trainers and got out running up hill and down dale around Much Wenlock. In 1982 he ran his first seven-mile race, followed by his first marathon the next year. By 2012 he had taken part in sixty marathons all over the world, competed in the London Marathon seventeen times, all proudly wearing his blue-and-white Wenlock Olympian vest. Amongst his highlights have been running marathons in Athens, on the original course, and along the Great Wall of China – and naturally being presented to the Queen on her visit to the games ground in 2003.

(See *Jimmy Moore Much Wenlock Marathon Man* on YouTube)

Seen here running along the Great Wall of China, Jimmy broke the course record for the China Marathon by 6 minutes.

Jimmy has held the record for the over-60s Ironbridge Half Marathon for four years. He is seen here crossing the famous Iron Bridge.

Jimmy holds an original 1948 Olympic torch aloft. He was the last runner in the relay team that had brought the torch from Bath to Much Wenlock in 1995 for the European Youth Olympics. The group are standing outside William Penny Brookes's house before the torch was taken into the church to rest overnight beneath the founder's memorial.

WOMEN AND CHILDREN INVITED TO TAKE PART

In the 1950 Centenary Games women were at last given the opportunity to compete; the 100 yards and 220 yards Ladies Flat Handicap appeared on the programme and attracted entries from clubs like Birmingham, West Bromwich, Halesowen and Birchfield Harriers. The following year 880 yards was added but it took until 1978 for athletics in the Olympian Games to really open up to women. From then on events for women have been added in response to demand and today most events have a women's junior, intermediate and senior category.

Children have always fared better in the Olympian Games than women, although in Brookes's day the races were for boys only. By the 1920s girls at the elementary schools in the Borough of Wenlock were invited to compete for the Borough Championship Shield in the 120 yards race, and there was a relay for them, but no further events were added, not even in the 1950s. The 1977 Silver Jubilee Games, however, were essentially for children and contained events like running 40 metres and swimming even for the under-6s. Throwing a rounders ball for girls and a cricket ball for boys in the 7–9 and 10–11 age groups was something Brookes would surely have recommended in his quest to improve the health of schoolchildren through PE. Events for junior classes have continued to expand ever since with the Wenlock Olympian Games being known for nurturing young talent.

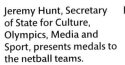
Shot putting for under-18 women came in in the late 1970s. Archery can be seen in the background.

Jeremy Hunt, Secretary of State for Culture, Olympics, Media and Sport, presents medals to the netball teams.

INTERNATIONAL RECOGNITION

'I came to pay tribute and homage to Dr Brookes who really was the founder of the Modern Olympic Games,' said the President of the IOC.

Four years after the Wenlock Olympians were visited by the President of the British Olympic Society HRH Princess Anne, His Excellency Juan Antonio Samaranch, the President of the International Olympic Committee, came to Much Wenlock. The year 1994 was the centenary of the founding of the International Olympic Committee, so the visit of the IOC President to the Wenlock Olympian Games was not just a great honour but accorded the Games international recognition for their role in the international Games. As Samaranch put it simply, 'I have come because this is where the Modern Olympics started.' He made a pilgrimage to Brookes's grave and laid a wreath.

During that same visit, Miss Joyce Farmer, ninety-two-year-old daughter of the 1891 tilting medal winner, presented the Wenlock Olympian Society with the original Coubertin medal her father had been awarded (see page 30).

His Excellency Juan Antonio Samaranch (left), President of the IOC, with Craig Reedie, Chairman of the BOA, and Dr Don Anthony.

Juan Antonio Samaranch, the President of the International Olympic Committee (centre), laid a wreath at the grave of Dr William Penny Brookes, recognising that this man was the inspiration for the modern Olympic Games. Craig Reedie (left),Chairman of the BOA and Norman Wood (right), the inspirational reviver of the 1977 Olympian Games, stand on either side.

An eminent gathering outside Much Wenlock museum which houses exhibits relating to the Olympian Games. Front row from left to right are Craig Reedie, Chairman of the British Olympic Association, Miss Farmer, whose father won the 1891 tilting, Juan Antonio Samaranch, President of the International Olympic Committee, Dr Don Anthony and back row Wenlock Olympian Committee members, Norman Wood and John Simpson.

71

EQUESTRIAN EVENTS

Equestrian events came and went from the Wenlock Olympian Games in the past but are now firmly established on the programme. Once Brookes's Games were running he introduced tilting (page 12) in 1858 as a crowd-pleaser, then a few years later notched up the excitement by making the riders jump hurdles before aiming for the ring. For a few years pony tilting was on the programme for the younger boys. In the 1890s a new horseback sport made a brief appearance on the programme: tent pegging. This clearly had a military origin because the rider was required to hurtle along the course and skewer a target on the ground with his sword or lance. An 1892 newspaper report described the outcry when Tom Rudd, described as 'undoubtedly the best tenter', was disqualified for not competing in his regimental uniform. The military slant continued in the early 1900s with costume racing for the yeomanry in 1909 (first prize a guinea) and, intriguingly, wrestling on horseback (a team event).

After the First World War equestrian events fell out of favour and vanished from the Games. In 1952 a gymkhana entered the Olympian Games programme with riders competing for the Wenlock Horse and Pony Gymkhana Cup. This event carried on for a few years.

In 2010 the Equestrian Event was introduced on the first Sunday of the Games and held at the Valley View near Broseley where there was plenty of space to compete. Showjumping is now held in two rings, a professional course-builder is employed and dressage takes place on an all-weather surface.

1910.
Wenlock Olympian Games
Whit-Tuesday May 17th.

Pony Races
(Catch weights)

Entrance Fee 5s. each event. About one and half miles.

Pony Race Committee:
Dr. Bigley, Messrs J. E. Boulton, E. Deakin, G. Lloyd, J. Moore, W. S, Tilley & A. Trevor
Judges:- Mr. W. Bishop & Dr. Hillyar.
Starter: Mr. W. R. Ainsworth.

4-0.   13-2 and under. First 50/-, Second £1.

1—Mr. Ed. Edwards'	...	...	NIMBLE KATE
2—Mr. Poole's	...	...	FLY
3—Mr. Dale's	...	...	FLY by NIGHT
4—Mr. F. Edwards'	...		CREEPING JENNY
5—Mrs. Massie's	...	...	BLACK BESS
6—Mr. Bethell's	...	...	DOLLY
7—Mr. J. Lloyd's	...	...	CREEPING DOLLY

5-5.   15-2 and under. First £4. Second £1.

1—Mr. W. T. Ainsworth's	...		WHEATLAND TRIXEY
2—Miss Edwards'	...	...	GOLDEN RAY
3—Dr. Hudson Bigley's	...		LEPRECHAUN
4—Mr. Dickenson's	...	...	TOMMY
5—Mr. W. E. C. Hutchings'	...	...	POLLY
6—Mr. W. Poole's	...	...	FLEA
7—Mr. F. Patrick's	...	...	POLLY
8—Mr. R. Jervis'	...	...	STOLEN KISS

N. B. Objections must be made within 15 minutes after the race. [1d]

Winners mount the podium
to receive their medals.

Jumping side-saddle
is no mean feat.

THE OLYMPIAN TRAIL

Visitors to Much Wenlock can often be seen, leaflet in hand, exploring the town and discovering the history of the Wenlock Olympian Games. The Olympian Trail was the culmination of a project that began in 1995, the hundredth anniversary of William Penny Brookes's death. Then titled the Much Wenlock Centennial Project, the aim was to celebrate the legacy and importance of Brookes's contribution to the town as well as his influence on the revival of the modern Olympic Games. Those involved wanted to create 'a suitable physically active tribute' that would help in the long-term economy of the town with tourism and marketing initiatives. Their solution? A walk around the town following bronze markers set in the ground to 'discover the sites and buildings associated with the Wenlock Olympian Story and learn about the benefits William Penny Brookes brought to the town during the 19th century'.

Lots of hard work and fund-raising later, the Olympian Trail was opened on Saturday 28 April 2001. Guests of honour were Paralympic gold medallist Debbie Brennan, Paralympic silver medallist Chris Hendy and Olympic bronze medallist, archer Alison Williamson, who joined a procession along the historic route the early Games had followed from the Gaskell Arms Hotel down the High Street.

Wenlock marathon runner ▶ Jimmy Moore carries the torch and stands behind Paralympic medallist Debbie Brennan.

▲
Following the route of the original games procession is Mayor Cllr Mrs Elizabeth Thomas, with Olympic medallists Debbie Brennan and Alison Williamson.

MUCH WENLOCK

Wenlock Olympian Society

"ARTE ET VIRIBUS"

SHROPSHIRE

Start at the Much Wenlock Museum near the town square in High Street. The trail begins and ends in the Museum, where a fine collection of Olympian artefacts is on display, illustrating the significant role of Much Wenlock in the revival of the modern Olympic Games.

Using your Trail Guide and Map follow the bronze markers set in the ground. Discover the sites and buildings associated with the Wenlock Olympian Story and learn about the benefits William Penny Brookes brought to the town during the 19th Century.

Parts of the Trail have limited access - please see Guide and Map. Walkers are advised that they follow the Trail at their own risk. The route crosses roads, footpaths, fields and steps.

Wenlock Olympian Trail commissioned in 2000, completed 2001

 Project part financed from European Regional Development Funds with Advantage West Midlands, Much Wenlock Town Council, Bridgnorth District Council, Millennium Festival Awards for All, Shropshire County Council and local sponsors.

RUNNING

Running has been in the Wenlock Games from the outset, with Brookes having two boys' races (for under-sevens and under-14s) and two men's races in the first Games. It has never lost its popularity, and more running events have been added with a full and a half marathon being included in the 2012 Games. Dress code has changed a little. Athletes in 1874 were told: 'If tights are worn, loose drawers round the loins must be worn.'

Kevin Evans is a fine example of one of Much Wenlock's home-grown talents. Inspired by Norman Wood to take up athletics when he was nine, Kevin was soon competing successfully for the Wenlock Olympians in track and field events, cross country and indoors, becoming under-15 1500m county champion. He continues to run in the Olympian Games today and had won the annual seven-mile race five times by 2011, as well as competing in Shropshire fell races and other off-road races. Like other Olympians, Kevin gives back to the society that nurtured him by assisting young athletes. Along with his partner Paula, he became team manager of the club's boys' events and a field official at meetings they attend, then in the late 1990s became a club coach, a task which he still does today, all of which puts Brookes's Olympian ideal into practice.

◀ Local athlete Chris Hill ran in the Wenlock Games as a schoolboy, then successfully completed the London Marathon for Mencap who supported his uncle Patrick (see page 55). When foot-and-mouth disease restricted Chris's training area, he ran from Much Wenlock to Craven Arms to work and back every day.

Kevin Evans wins the cup for the seven-mile race in 2011 for the fifth year. He says, 'My daughter Katie is keen on running. I hope she will take after me!'
▼

▲ By 2012 entries for the seven-mile road race were over two hundred and fifty. Kevin Evans can be seen wearing number 115.

SHOOTING

Shooting did have a place in Brookes's Games for a short period. It was largely in response to the Crimean War and the fear of a French invasion which haunted the country in the late 1850s. In 1859 the government set up the Volunteer Rifle Corps, a sort of local part-time defence body. In response to this in the 1860s the Wenlock Olympian Games introduced rifle shooting as one of its events. The rifle shooting took place a little way out of town at Blakeway on the Church Stretton road near the Horse & Jockey pub always referred to by locals as 'The Bonnets'.

Competitive rifle shooting only lasted a few years, but shooting returned to the Olympian Games in 1990 in the form of clay pigeon shooting. In homely fashion, the Secretary knew that Bill Jones, a friend from neighbouring Bourton, had his own trap because he used it once a year to raise funds for the old people's Christmas party. Bill offered to run the shoot for the Society and the Games's first clay pigeon shoot was held on the Sunday afternoon at the Cutlins, a field next to the Priory ruins. Complaints about the noise later led to the transfer of the shoot to a farm at nearby Callaughton where it continues today.

WENLOCK OLYMPIAN GAMES.

THE RIFLE SHOOTING will **TAKE PLACE** at **BLAKEWAY, NEAR WENLOCK**, on **TUESDAY, AUGUST 21st.**

FOR RIFLE SHOOTING : Prize, to the best Marksman belonging to any of the Shropshire Rifle Volunteer Corps, a Silver Cup, value £12 12s. Entrance fee, 2s. 6d. Intending competitors to send in their names to Mr. W. P. Brookes, Wenlock, together with a certificate of their fitness to contend, signed by a commissioned officer of their corps, on or before Friday, August 17th. The competition will take place on Tuesday, August 21st, at Blakeway, near Much Wenlock. Range, 300 and 500 yards, at two targets, with bull's eye and centre ring. The competitors will meet at the Corn Market at nine o'clock a.m. and proceed in a body to the shooting ground. Red flags will be placed to indicate danger. The Cup will be presented to the successful competitor at the Luncheon on Wednesday, the 22nd, by Lieut. Col. Sir Herbert B. Edwardes. Regulations for the competition will be drawn up by Captain T. C. Eyton, 7th Shropshire Rifles.

To the Second Best Shot among the Competitors for the Silver Cup, a Short Enfield Rifle, complete with Sword, &c. presented by the Right Hon. Lord Berwick.

◀ This newspaper report shows the prizes for rifle shooting in the 1860s were impressive.

SOME TEAM GAMES

Bowling always enjoyed a thriving life in Much Wenlock but didn't feature in Brookes's Games apart from in 1872. During his day the green was used as the dance floor at the end of the Games and in 1902 '500 school children were supplied with tea on the bowling green' and in 1909 the Jackfield Brass Band performed on the green. However from the 1920s competitive bowling has been part of the Games and has continued ever since.

Fortunately competitors have not been put off by this advice from local businessman T.H. Thompson in 1901:

> A few words about the kind of players you see in a bowling club. You sometimes see a few younger people who perhaps cannot join a cricket or tennis club or perhaps too lazy to exert themselves at these two games. Taken on the whole the majority of members are old stagers, men who have passed their cricketing and tennis days; men who still cling to the outdoor pastime of our country for the love of sport, and for the sake of health.

Cricket was present in Brookes's first Games but died out in the mid 1860s probably because it took too long to complete a game. Since then there have been invitation cricket matches as part of the Games and eight-a-side kwik cricket. Throwing the cricket ball continues to be an Olympian sport for under-11 boys with under-11 girls throwing a rounders ball. Other team sports in the Games include tennis, badminton, netball, hockey and football.

OTHER SPORTS

Workers in the limestone quarries on Wenlock Edge had their own event called 'putting the limestone' which involved pitching a 35lb hunk of rock. It was usually the lads from Lea Quarry versus the lads from the Shadwell Quarry, but the closure of Shadwell put an end to the sport. Although revived in the recent past, this is not an event on today's programme.

The 25-metre swimming pool heated by solar panels in the new William Brookes School has put the Masters Swimming Gala back in the Olympian Games and enabled swimming to be part of the triathlon. ▶

Cycling is a part of the triathlon and attracts many competitors.
▼

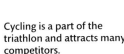

THE WENLOCK PENTATHLON

The pentathlon was popular when first introduced in Brookes's day but had a slightly chequered history in the 1880s. It was still in the Games in the early 1920s when Cecil Nevett was competing (see page 34–5) but dropped from the programme a year or so later as interest once again dwindled. It did not reappear for a long time. In 1980, the centenary year of the AAA, its President Mr Squire Yarrow, asked the Wenlock Olympian Society if they would restart the Senior Men's Pentathlon. The Society was more than happy to oblige and added a women's category as well. The Wenlock Pentathlon, as it was known, proved so popular that a Boys, Girls, Inter-Ladies and Youth category quickly followed. The sports in the Wenlock Pentathlon are 800 metres, hurdles, shot put, long jump and high jump. Fortunately for some, Brookes's earlier 55-foot rope climb was not an event that was revived!

A Triathlon Championship was introduced in the 1990 Games comprising a 500-metre swim, 15-kilometre bike ride and a six-kilometre cross country run. By 2011 the cross country distance had increased to 17 kilometres and the bike ride to 19 kilometres. The same year a junior biathlon with a swimming and running event were also introduced.

◀ A 19-kilometre bike ride is part of the triathlon.

NORMAN WOOD
(1921-2005)

The present Wenlock Olympian Society owes its revival and survival to the efforts of a number of people, but everyone agrees that without Norman Wood it would never have happened. In many ways he was the modern counterpart to William Penny Brookes, an inspiration and a worker who made things happen.

After the Second World War, spent, he said, eating and sleeping in the back of a truck for three-and-a-half years supplying parts for a tank unit, Norman went into teaching. He arrived in Much Wenlock in 1953 at the newly-built secondary school at one end of the games field. As head of PE he set up football, athletics, cross country, cricket and tennis teams. Later he moved to run adult education in the Bridgnorth area where he organised all manner of courses from modern languages to choral music: one of his enduring legacies is the Much Wenlock Male Voice Choir.

Norman was always aware of the demise of the once famous Wenlock Olympian Society and wanted to revive it. In 1977, when he was mayor, he restarted the Wenlock Olympian Society and their annual Games to celebrate the Queen's Silver Jubilee (see pages 50-1). Never content to be just a figurehead Norman was active in forming clubs like athletics

and fencing, managing teams, coaching and above all inspiring people to join him. His wife Barbara was equally busy behind the scenes rallying supporters, baking cakes for the freezer all year, then selling them on games day to raise money for the Society.

Norman's enthusiasm and commitment to the Wenlock Olympian Society was recognised in 2003 when he was presented to the Queen and Prince Philip. The strength and survival of the Wenlock Olympian Society and its Games are largely down to one man and his belief that 'anything is possible'.

◀ In 2006 when the 2012 Roadshow came to Much Wenlock, the British Olympic Association presented the Wenlock Olympian Society with a trophy in honour of Norman Wood in recognition of his life-long contribution to sport. The trophy is awarded annually by the Olympian Society to the person who has contributed the most to the Wenlock Olympian Games.

Norman Wood as PE teacher at the newly-built Much Wenlock County Secondary School in 1953.
▼

It was fitting that Norman Wood should be presented to the Queen in 2003 during her visit to Much Wenlock along with the Mayoress Mrs Jean Childs.

DEDICATED SUPPORTERS

The success of the Wenlock Olympian Society and its Games has been down to the loyal support of many, many people from Brookes's time to the present day. Some have been visible at the side of the track assisting with the Games, others have worked behind the scenes. Over the years there have been jobs like receiving the hundreds of entries, sorting them and handwriting lists (in pre-computer days); or going out on the field the night before the Games to set it up by hammering in wooden posts and attaching pig wire to separate spectators from competitors; or baking cakes and making sandwiches to feed the officials on the day and to sell to the public. There is also the work that goes on all year in the different clubs that make up the Wenlock Olympian Society, helping people enjoy sport and nurturing young talent.

It was fitting that in 2008 the Wenlock Olympian Society was awarded The Queen's Award for Voluntary Service in recognition of the dedication people have put into the Society over the years.

▲
In 2006 the Norman Wood Trophy was given to the Wenlock Olympian Society by the British Olympic Association. Roy Rogers, President of the Wenlock Olympian Society, received the trophy from Jonathan Edwards.

▲
Members of the Wenlock Olympian Society received The
Queen's Award for Voluntary Service which recognises excellence
in voluntary activities carried out by groups in the community.

**The Queen's Award
for Voluntary Service**

The MBE for volunteer groups

89

WENLOCK GREETS THE LONDON 2012 OLYMPICS

August 24, 2008 marked the official handover of the Olympic Games from Beijing to London and the start of the journey towards the London 2012 Olympic and Paralympic Games. It was a great honour for the Wenlock Olympian Society to have been chosen to raise one of the official Olympic Handover Flags because all the other flags had been given to governmental bodies.

Crowds turned out to celebrate the raising of the flag and even 'the doctor' put in a special appearance. Appropriately attired in Victorian costume and complete with his Olympian medals, 'Dr Brookes' led a procession of dancing girls down the High Street to the Guildhall to watch the flag-raising. Then he moved on to stand on the steps of his house in Wilmore Street where he is seen greeting the Town Crier (on loan from Wellington, Telford, because Much Wenlock doesn't have one).

On 19 May 2010 representatives of London 2012, including Jonathan Edwards, came to Much Wenlock to announce details of the Olympic mascots. What took everyone's breath away was when he announced that the Olympic mascot was to be called *Wenlock* to honour the town's importance in the revival of the modern Olympics. *Mandeville* would be the name of the Paralympic mascot in recognition of the Stoke Mandeville Games as the forerunner of the Paralympics. That production of these mascot toys would go to Shropshire firm Golden Bear Products was an added bonus for the county. One of *Wenlock's* first public appearances was on Sunday 11 July 2010 at the Wenlock Olympian Games and this provoked great interest on the field. There was some speculation that his outfit might still be in the early stages of production because *Wenlock* appeared only able to waddle short strides and was heavily reliant on his guide to see where he was going!

None of that dampened enthusiasm for this celebrity appearance, nor for the honour awarded the town by the Olympic mascot carrying its name.

Wenlock proved a big draw when he appeared at the 2010 Olympian Games.

The official 2012 flag was raised on the Guildhall to show the Olympics had moved from Beijing to London.

◀ 'The doctor' greets the Town Crier on the steps of the Brookes family home in 2010.

THE OLYMPIC IMPACT

The small market town of Much Wenlock with a population of barely 3,000 was delighted when their Games and its founding father Dr William Penny Brookes were recognised as having played such a significant part in the modern Olympic movement. Fame has brought many famous faces to the town to pay homage to Dr William Penny Brookes and to watch the Wenlock Olympian Games. Once it was known that London would host the 2012 Olympics, media interest in Much Wenlock increased massively with journalists and film crews from around the world descending on the place. In some ways the little town may wonder what has hit them but in other ways they are extremely proud of their heritage and pleased to share it with the world.

▲ MP Jeremy Hunt, the Secretary of State for Culture, Olympics, Media and Sport, was the guest of honour in 2011. He is standing with 'the doctor', appropriately enough Dr Jim Wentel, one of the doctors in the Much Wenlock Medical Practice and athlete himself.

◀ Tony Robinson arrived in Much Wenlock in 2011 with an Australian television crew to film the town and the Games.

David Ottley congratulates the medallists.
▼

A BRIGHT FUTURE

In 2012, the year of the London Olympic Games, the Wenlock Olympian Games are stronger than ever. Like William Penny Brookes, the present-day organisers of the Games have their sights set on the future and in 2012 will offer Olympic gliding as an event. Gliding was indeed an Olympic sport on the programme of the 1936 Berlin Games, but disappeared because of the Second World War and has yet to return.

Other new events for the Wenlock Games in 2012 are the marathon, half marathon and the Wenlock Olympian 100-mile walk. Continuing William Penny Brookes's concern to develop the mind as well as the body, the town will also host a group of disabled artists as part of the London 2012 Cultural Olympiad.

With 2012 being the 126th Wenlock Olympian Games, it is clear Brookes's creation has a long and bright future. The vision of one man in 1850 has been successfully carried forward by many, many hardworking volunteers over the years, to whom this book is dedicated.

A silver Olympic flame rises from a map of the world in the Olympian sculpture that was unveiled on the Linden Field in 2011 by Mayor Cllr Lesley Durbin. The sculpture was created by Shropshire designer and metalworker Adrian Reynolds and has an inscription 'his imagination a worldwide inspiration' around the map as a tribute to William Penny Brookes.
▼

ACKNOWLEDGEMENTS

We are grateful for all the help given us by members of the community in and around Much Wenlock who shared their own experiences of the Wenlock Olympian Games and recalled what older friends and relatives had told them. This has been a vital source of information.

We are also very grateful for the kind assistance of the Wenlock Olympian Society and in particular Chris Cannon and Peter Thompson who have given us many hours of helpful advice and guidance. We are also grateful to the Wenlock Olympian Society for allowing us to reproduce material from their archive and for Paul Nichols for helping us access them. The Society's pictures appear on pages 8, 9, 10, 11, 12, 16, 22, 23, 24, 25, 26, 27, 29, 30, 31, 34, 42, 43, 45, 46, 47, 49, 53, 55, 58, 59, 62, 65, 67, 71, 72, 74, 82, 86, 88, 89 and 91.

Emma-Kate Lanyon from Shropshire Museum Service helped us find information and allowed us to turn up at odd, and probably inconvenient, times to locate photographs and check facts without ever complaining. Thank you. Shropshire Museum Service's photographs appear on pages 13, 15, 17, 18, 19, 20, 21, 32, 34, 35 and 63.

Thanks are also due to Much Wenlock Town Council for their kind permission to reproduce their painting on page 14 and for allowing us to work in their archives. Special thanks must also go to Howard Horsley, Honorary Archivist, who gave up his time to assist us with research in the archives.

We are very grateful to Sabine Hutchinson of Virtual Shropshire for allowing us to reproduce her wonderful action photographs of the modern Wenlock Olympian Games which appear on pages 23, 45, 46, 61, 68, 69, 73, 76, 77, 78, 79, 80, 81, 82, 83, 84, 85, 86, 87, 91, 92, 93, 94 and 95.

All other photographs have been kindly loaned from private collections.

Writing this book has been enormous fun for us all and we are well aware that it could not have been achieved without the help of everyone. A big thank you!

Two other recently published books that give an insight into the Wenlock Olympian Games are:

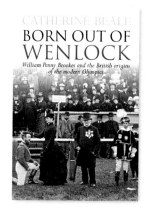

Available from online from www.cbeale.co.uk and at most bookshops

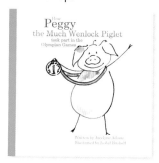

This illustrated children's book tells the story of the first Wenlock Olympian Games through the eyes of a piglet and is available online from www.ellinghampress.co.uk and at most bookshops